TEACH AND BE RICH

AN EDUCATOR'S FINANCIAL HANDBOOK

Michael Franzblau, Ph.D.

Pinebrook
Press

This publication is designed to provide accurate information in regard to its subject matter. The information it contains has been carefully researched, and all efforts have been made to ensure accuracy as of the date published. The publisher sells this book with the understanding that it is not engaged in rendering legal, accounting, insurance or other professional services. The publisher does not intend this book to serve as an investment guide. The book contains no specific investment advice. The information contained in this book should by no means be considered as a substitute for competent professional advice. The reader should not use the contents of this book as the basis for purchasing specific investments or insurance products without the reader first consulting a competent independent professional advisor. Before making any decision or taking action based on the information or strategies contained in this book, the reader should seek the services of a competent professional advisor.

For information about bulk sales or to use this book as a fundraiser for an educator association, contact *groupsales@pinebrookpress.com.*

Book Layout and Cover Design by Richard A. Miller

ISBN 0-910859-18-3

Library of Congress Control Number: 2003095968

Printed in the United States of America

Acknowledgements:

Many people have contributed to this book over the five years it took me to complete it.

For ongoing support and countless excellent suggestions, I thank my wife Mollyann. She helped me keep on writing when the task seemed endless, and reminded me that the creative process requires that one let go of the finished product. • For constant coaching and encouragement over the years: Mark and Cressida Franzblau, Lauren and Darren Renner, Robin Franzblau, Peter Levy, Joan and Art Nowick, Alice Nagel, Sarah Nagel, and Reuben Spenser. • Daniel Solicito helps me implement these strategies with educators every day, and constantly expands and improves them. • Many friends and colleagues from Strategies for Wealth Creation and Protection added to this book. Jerry Harnik carefully read this manuscript and made many significant improvements. Ron Rosbruch, Josh Becker, David Bibcoff, Peter Adams and Andrew Brown guided and encouraged me throughout the lengthy process of writing and rewriting. Diane Finch sheparded the manuscript through the compliance process that verifies its accuracy. • Thomas Meehan gave me expert advice on long-term care insurance policies and checked this portion of the text. • Michael Leo, Esq. gave me his encouragement as well as his expert legal advice. Andrew Abrams and Marc Schwaber provided ongoing support and inspiration. • Anthony DiCarlo, Dr. Thomas Higgins, Dr. Melvin Imas, Dr. William C. Prattella, Betty Fisch, Dr. Robert Maher and Shirley Gilwit took time to carefully read and comment on the book. • Larry Prince helped with the formatting and computer graphics. • Suzan Russell, Ph.D. edited the manuscript and suggested many important changes, which greatly improved this book. • Richard A. Miller designed the interior layout and the cover. His expertise made complex information easier to understand.

TABLE OF CONTENTS

PREFACE   1

Discover what you really want in your life, and how to achieve it
Micro and macro planning: You have got to do both
Take the time to construct and review your plan
Look at all the possibilities before acting
Consider exit strategies before you begin investing

CHAPTER ONE   9

INTRODUCTION
When should you begin to plan for retirement?
Financial goals in retirement
Managing financial risks
The survivorship option-a critical choice
Long-term healthcare planning
Investment Planning
Estate Planning

CHAPTER TWO   17

MANAGING FINANCIAL RISKS
Property and casualty insurance: protecting what you own
Types of P&C policies
You need to understand the insurance contract
More about liability limits and deductibles
Replacing your earning potential for your family
Disability income protection insurance
What happens to you family's lifestyle if you die tomorrow?
Qualifying for private insurance: the underwriting process
What kind of life insurance should I purchase?

TABLE OF CONTENTS

The components of a permanent life insurance policy
Whole life insurance
Universal life insurance
Variable whole life insurance
Variable universal life insurance
How much life insurance is
sufficient to replace my income?
Long-term care insurance
Federal and state programs for long-term care
Long-term care insurance: a solution

CHAPTER THREE   **59**

HOW YOUR PENSION REALLY WORKS
Pension basics
Pension options
Consequences of taking maximum pension
Period certain and survivorship options: passing your pension on
        after your death
What kind of life insurance should I purchase?
When should you purchase life insurance for pension protection?
How do you select the right insurance company?
How will you pay the premiums in retirement?
Should you plan to use the cash value as a retirement supplement?
How time may enhance the survivor's pension
Who should own the life insurance contract?
Purchasing life insurance inside your 403(b) tax sheltered annuity plan

CHAPTER FOUR   **105**

HOW TO ORGANIZE AN INVESTMENT STRATEGY
FOR YOUR RETIREMENT
Why you may need to plan for an ever-increasing family income
Other economic forces that affect retirement income

The role your investments will play
Creating an investment strategy
Modern portfolio/efficient market theory
How to live with a volatile market
The role of income and dividends
Is now a good time to invest?
More lessons from history
Buying during the sale
Dollar Cost Averaging
The role of diversification in designing your portfolio
Designing portfolios with low volatility
Sample portfolios for different investor goals
Mutual funds
What does it cost to purchase and own a mutual fund?
Taxation of gains in a mutual fund

CHAPTER FIVE   139

HOW TO PLAN YOUR ESTATE

Why pay attention to estate planning?
How estates are taxed
The probate prrocess
Popular estate planning strategies
The simple will
Revocable and Irrevocable trusts
The Pour-over Will
The QTIP Trust
The Qualified Domestic Trust
The Living Will
The Durable Power of Attorney
The Credit Shelter Trust
The Irrevocable Life Insurance Trust for a married couple
Charitable bequests
Second-To-Die Life Insurance policies

TABLE OF CONTENTS

AFTERWORD 164

APPENDIX A 169

INFORMATION YOUR PLANNER WILL REQUIRE

APPENDIX B 173

HOW MEDICARE AND MEDICAID WORK
Medicare
Medicaid
Medicaid "look back" rules
Can you make your assets inaccessible to Medicaid?
What about Medicaid-avoidance trusts?
Is your home safe from Medicaid?

APPENDIX C 181

AN OVERVIEW OF SOCIAL SECURITY BENEFITS
Eligibility
Benefit calculation
Early retirement
Reviewing your Earnings and Benefits Statement
Spousal and family benefits
Other benefits
Social Security taxes
Taxation of Social Security benefits

FOOTNOTES 189

ABOUT THE AUTHOR 195

INDEX 197

LIST OF FIGURES

FIGURE 1   37
Relationship between the components of a permanent life insurance policy

FIGURE 2   56
Maximum tax deduction for qualified long-term-care premiums at various ages

FIGURE 3   81
Joint and survivor options for John and Molly retiring at age 60

FIGURE 4   88
Returns from various asset categories from 1/1/1970 to 12/31/1999

FIGURE 5   108
Increasing income required to maintain purchasing power under 4% inflation

FIGURE 6   118
100 years of stock market declines

FIGURE 7   120
Investing for the short or long term

FIGURE 8   128
Returns and the risks investors took to get them

FIGURE 9   129
Time frame and risk tolerance for different investor goals

FIGURE 10   130
Sample investment mixes

FIGURE 11   144
Federal gift and estate tax for 2003

FIGURE 12   182
Normal retirement age for Social Security benefits

PREFACE

When I was a teacher, I never expected to become a financial specialist to educators. Originally, trained as a physicist, I spent a decade in scientific research before realizing I would rather teach than practice physics. Just after my 30th birthday, a month after my wife and I bought our first house, the industrial research laboratory where I worked closed and I lost my job. In that year many research scientists I knew in private industry suffered the same fate and had to find other careers. I had always enjoyed explaining my work to anyone who would listen, and so I thought I would try teaching. The next day I walked into the high school in the small town I had just moved to, and asked them if I could teach science. Because I had some college teaching experience and had earned a doctorate in materials science at Yale, I was hired on the spot. I told the superintendent that I had no background in education and he gave me five years to earn the education credits that I needed for my teaching license.

I spent the next twenty years teaching a variety of sciences, and for the most part, I enjoyed every day. In my second year of teaching, I became the coordinator of an experimental alternative high school, which became a national model.

In my early years as a teacher, money was a problem in our family, for we had decided that my wife would not return to work until our kids were older. Like many educators feeling a money pinch, I decided to take a second job. I looked at many possibilities and decided that the field of financial services might work for me. Within a few weeks of making this choice, I received an unsolicited letter from a large insurance company inviting me to become a financial representative. I accepted their offer. After months of rigorous training in the early hours of the morning and several license exams, I learned enough to go to work. I chose to work with public educators because I understood our common problems and challenges. I decided to market my services by presenting informational seminars to interested educators. After several months, I learned to convey my message clearly from a podium and I developed a steady clientele with New York area teachers and administrators. I was delighted to discover that teaching educators how to make better money decisions was as satisfying as teaching high school students physics.

I juggled both careers for five years, working until 3:30pm at the high school and then from 4:00pm until 11:00pm at the homes of educators. In my twentieth year as a teacher I decided to retire and devote my time and efforts to my financial planning business.

In this book I have tried to relate what I have learned in the last eighteen years about building and protecting wealth, in a way that every educator can potentially apply to his or her own financial circumstances. Much of the information is technical and some will be familiar, since we all deal with money issues every day. I believe that every educator can become financially successful even though educators typically do not earn as much as they deserve to.

I hope that this book will give you the tools and knowledge which will enable you to live a more than financially comfortable life.

Decide what you really want in your life, and how to achieve it.

Imagine yourself three years in the future. Ask yourself this question: "What has to have happened during those three years for me to be happy about my financial situation?" Be as specific as you can. For example, do you want to someday have a vacation home?

What are you willing to do *now* to make this happen in the near future? What are you not willing to do? What specific obstacles will you have to overcome? How can you enjoy the process of conquering these obstacles? What opportunities do you have at this moment that can help you achieve your goal? What talents and strengths do you bring to this challenge? If you are working with a planner, tell him or her about your financial dreams, and make sure he or she understands what is most important to you about money. Use your planner to help you get what you want in the future *right now*.

Micro and macro planning:
You have to do both.

The micro planning approach looks closely at each asset to make sure it is sufficient for its purpose. For example, micro planning examines your life insurance policies to make sure that the owner, beneficiary, and insured are correctly listed. The macro approaches also focuses on how these policies link with and reinforce other assets. Each asset has this micro and macro aspect, and both are important. The macro approach views all of your financial assets as part of your "family economy," and is concerned with how efficiently your economy functions. After you are sure that every financial component is working smoothly, step back and make sure all the parts are working together.

Take the time to construct and review
your plan.

You will be retired for a long time, possibly thirty-five years. This amounts to more than 300,000 hours. In contrast, you need only devote ten to twenty hours a year constructing and reviewing your financial plan. You will benefit greatly from this effort. Your life will be free of financial worries, and your heirs will be grateful that you spent the time to do things right.

Look at all the possibilities before acting.

There are many financial products and strategies for you to use in your personal financial economy. Each will have advantages and disadvantages. You have a better chance of making the right choice if you analyze as many alternatives as possible. Be creative: look for new and better ideas. For example, have you ever heard of a reverse mortgage? Most people are unaware that new financial strategies are being created all the time. Your planner should update you on new and potentially useful strategies. And since you are more familiar with your situation than any planner, do not be afraid to trust your instincts when evaluating alternatives.

Consider exit strategies before you begin investing.

Plan how you will get out of a financial strategy before you get in. Many financial strategies and products at first may appear beneficial. However, upon further examination you may realize that these strategies and products may cause you problems down the road. A tax-sheltered annuity is an example. Educators who make annual tax-deferred deposits into 403(b) plans enjoy the current deferral on earned income that they invest in their plans. However, they must pay the deferred taxes on the annual deposits plus the deferred taxes on the growth in the plan (if any) when money is withdrawn. They may discover that they are in a *higher* tax bracket when they are ready to withdraw money from their 403(b) account than when they deferred the deposits. Now is a good time to ask your planner whether you can create an offsetting tax deduction when you begin to withdraw money.

When you are ready to implement a financial strategy, make sure that you have considered how you will access your money with minimum tax impact when the time comes to cash in.

CHAPTER 1

INTRODUCTION

Why are so few Americans financially successful? You may have heard the financial service industry's standard answer: *Most people do not plan to fail; they fail to plan.* And yet, even if we take time to plan, it does not always work to our advantage.

You have many sources of information when you begin to plan for your retirement. Your state pension system may provide you with an updated employment benefit statement each year, which in some states gives you a projection of your potential pension benefit. By using simple arithmetic formulas that take into account your potential salary increases, you can estimate with reasonable accuracy the amount of your pension benefit. But as we will see, there is more to retirement planning than knowing how large your pension may be. Many educators feel their pensions and health benefits provide all the security they will need in retirement. Not necessarily so! What seems an adequate income at retirement may shrink in spending power over time if ongoing inflation compounds the cost of living. Do you remember how much you were paid as an educator twenty years ago? How far would that salary go today? Besides inflation, you must take into account the many risks that threaten your financial well being, or you will find yourself worrying about money in later years.

When should you begin to plan for retirement?

The earlier, the better. You may still be early in your career or retirement may have crept up on you. Either way, you must ask yourself certain questions. Do you know when you can afford to retire? Will you be able to maintain your lifestyle over decades of inflationary pressures? Should you worry about outliving your resources? While it is ideal to start planning as early as possible, it is never too late.

For some, retirement means the chance to do those things that they did not have the time or the money to do while they were working. For others, it is an anxious phase of life. Whatever our circumstances, our ability to move forward with confidence improves as we take time to plan. Yet, many people do not plan due to time constraints or the human tendency to put off what seems difficult. The sooner you examine your needs and your options, the more opportunities will be available to you. The earlier you investigate all the possibilities, the greater the likelihood of achieving your goals.

Financial goals in retirement.

During the last fifteen years I have spoken with more than a thousand educators, who have in one form or another expressed these retirement goals: They want a comfortable retirement, and do not want to worry about having to limit their lifestyle should they live a very long time. They want to have the financial capability to help their children should the need arise, and to provide for the education of their grandchildren. If their parents should need financial assistance, they would like to be able to provide it. Many want to leave a legacy to an institution they admire, such as a charity, school, religious organization or another worthy cause.

It takes a lot of money to achieve these goals. It also takes commitment to a process in which you must begin now, and continue to actively participate throughout your retirement. By beginning this process now, you can make the most of what you have in order to achieve what you want. You can identify needs and explore options for achieving both short and long-term goals. You can examine the tax implications of various decisions. You can develop approaches that reconcile your financial needs with your personal tolerance for risk. Your reward: peace of mind and financial security.

Managing financial risks.

No matter what the future brings, you need to take steps to assure that you and your family will be financially secure. Risk management is the process of protecting yourself, your family and your wealth from all possible risks. It is an essential but often overlooked part of a plan. Many people live with decisions that they made passively, by letting things slide. Believing that they have lots of time to plan later on, they leave themselves and their families vulnerable to events that can destroy their economic stability. What could go wrong with your financial plan?

Unfortunately, many things. For instance, you could die prematurely. Or you could lose your ability to work because of an illness or accident that causes a long-term disability. As you grow older, a long-term care need could wipe out your savings. You could be sued and your assets taken away. You could lose your wealth through poor investments.

The survivorship option: a critical choice.

Most educators do not understand how their pension system works, and how it can work against them. Every state teachers retirement system poses a tough choice to its members. Assume that there is someone in your life who will survive you, and whom you love more than your pension system. This intended beneficiary of your pension could be a spouse, a child, grandchildren, a charity or an institution. Suppose the beneficiary is your spouse. When you near retirement you have to decide whether to opt for the maximum pension and leave no pension for your spouse at your death, or choose a reduced pension that at your death leaves a smaller share to your spouse. The latter choice results in an annual pension reduction that can destroy a quarter of your pension. By choosing a survivorship option, in most states you surrender the right to change your designated beneficiary should that individual predecease or divorce you. If your spouse dies first, your pension continues at the reduced level. Nothing passes on to your heirs. There are more flexible ways to protect your survivor, and you should address them well before you retire. Those educators who have planned properly may enjoy more money in retirement and be able to pass more to their heirs than those who did not take time to plan.

Long-term healthcare planning.

By age 65, you have more than a 50% likelihood of needing three years of long-term care services at some point in the future.[1] Long-term care is very expensive and is not covered by most major medical plans. Although the cost varies greatly across the nation, nursing homes in the New York metropolitan area charge a daily rate of approximately $300 per day or more than $100,000 annually. Home care ranges from hundreds to thousands of dollars a month. The expense can be disastrous for anyone. Fortunately, long-term care insurance policies are available at reasonable cost, and can protect you from financial ruin. Although these policies have improved in recent years, they are complicated to understand and filled with options you must select. If you do not understand how they work, you could easily pay more for less coverage. The Taxpayer Reform Act of 1997 created tax benefits for purchasers of long-term care policies, making it easier to pay for coverage. If you learn how to analyze the coverage, costs and the financial soundness of insurers, you can select a policy best suited for your situation.

Investment Planning.

The nineties saw a proliferation of mutual funds, equities, new kinds of investment-related insurance policies, and other financial instruments. Some are excellent, many risky. Short-term needs require different strategies from long-term needs, yet both are important. You would be wise to consider the tax implications when making investment decisions that will impact your retirement.

Estate Planning.

Will you have an estate to pass on to your heirs? How hard will it be hit by taxes? Under current law, estate taxes were reduced beginning in 2002 and are currently scheduled to disappear entirely in 2010, only to reappear in 2011 at 2001 levels. Proper estate planning can slash your family's estate tax bill, but it can do much more. It can help assure that your assets pass to the right people at the right time. You need to have the right types of wills and trusts for your specific circumstances. Powers of attorney can protect you in case of incapacity. Organizing your estate can seem a daunting task, but understanding your choices will make it easier. Consult with your attorney or tax specialist to learn how estate tax laws pertain to your specific situation.

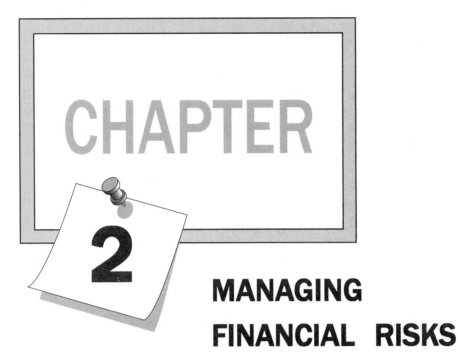

MANAGING FINANCIAL RISKS

Each of us can utilize a variety of legal arrangements and insurance products designed to protect our wealth in the event of a mishap, lawsuit or disaster. The insurance products include car and home insurance, personal liability insurance, medical insurance, disability income protection insurance, long-term care insurance and life insurance. The legal arrangements include wills and trusts and insurance ownership arrangements. It is crucially important that you organize these parts of your financial life so that your assets will be safe if you have an automobile accident, a liability suit, an untimely death or a disability.

Keep in mind that insurance is intended to replace the full value of the insured item, whether property, income or human life value. Insurance protects you best when it provides complete replacement of whatever was lost.

> Insurance is intended to replace the full value of the insured item.

Property and casualty insurance: protecting what you own.

"Property and casualty" (P&C) is the term commonly used to describe insurance designed to protect an individual from loss or damage to the physical assets he or she owns. For example, a fire may seriously damage or even completely destroy a home. If you do not have adequate homeowner's insurance to provide the funds to repair or rebuild, such a loss could be a financial disaster. Homeowners' policies can also provide protection for the home's contents, such as furniture, appliances, and other personal belongings. P&C policies can also provide "liability" protection. For example, if your automobile causes an accident, you may be required by a court (be found "liable") to pay others for repair of property damage, medical expenses, lost wages or "pain and suffering." The judgments may be large and could seriously affect your future financial security.

Types of P&C policies.

Property and casualty policies come in many forms and cover a wide spectrum of risks. Additional coverage, called endorsements, can be added to a basic policy to provide protection against risks found only in certain geographical areas, to protect specific types of property, or to cover a temporary situation. Some of the most common types of policies and endorsements include:

Automobile insurance:

If you own or operate a car, you are exposed to serious financial risk. Your personal liability arising from losses suffered by others, bodily injury or the cost of repairing or replacing a damaged or stolen vehicle, can be very high. Automobile insurance covers these risks. It affords you liability protection in case you are sued. Most states compel owners of motor vehicles to maintain liability insurance as a condition of licensing or to use public roadways. Your state may require owners of vehicles to prove their "financial responsibility" before and after an accident.

The most frequently used policy for private passenger automobiles is the personal automobile policy (PAP), sometimes called a "package policy." The PAP can be extended to cover other types of vehicles. The PAP typically includes:

Liability insurance to protect the owner against losses from legal liability arising from bodily injury or property damage caused by an automobile accident. Coverage can be either a single limit, (say, $100,000 for each accident), or split limits such as $50,000/ $100,000/ $25,000 (per person/per accident for bodily injury/ property damage).

Physical damage coverage pays for physical damage to the insured auto. Collision covers losses arising from colliding vehicles.

Medical payments coverage pays medical or funeral expenses arising from bodily injury. The coverage ranges in increments of $1,000 to $5,000 up to $10,000 per person per accident.

Comprehensive ("other than collision") coverage protects you from losses from risks not connected to a collision, such as theft, fire or storm damage. Losses for physical damage are measured by the cost to repair or replace the damaged or stolen vehicle.

Uninsured/underinsured motorist: Even though many states have enacted "financial responsibility" laws, many automobile owners ignore these laws and do not purchase insurance. *Uninsured* motorist coverage pays for injuries sustained in an accident with an uninsured (or a hit-and-run) driver. *Underinsured* motorist insurance covers the gap, if any, between the actual losses sustained, and the amount of money the insured motorist can collect from an at-fault driver, up to the policy limit.

Homeowner's insurance:

Every homeowner is exposed to both potential losses and personal liability. Your home, together with its contents, is typically the largest asset on the family "balance sheet." A homeowner could be financially ruined if he or she lost their home and its contents to theft, fire, a windstorm, or some other disaster. Even the partial destruction of one's home, if not protected by insurance, could bring financial devastation. Beyond these losses, the homeowner is exposed to substantial liability. For example, a visitor could slip or fall and sustain a serious injury. Lawsuits arising from such incidents may result in large awards to the injured party for medical expenses, and punitive damages for "pain and suffering." A homeowner's insurance policy provides protection for the homeowner against a wide range of losses and personal liability coverage.

Make sure that your policy covers "replacement cost." If your home is damaged or totally destroyed, your policy will either pay (within policy limits) to rebuild or repair on an "actual cash value" basis, or you will be reimbursed on a "replacement cost" basis. The latter affords you better protection. Actual cash value means the difference between replacement cost and an amount for depreciation or for wear and tear. Coverage based on actual cash value could leave you short of the total funds needed to restore your home. A replacement cost policy, while somewhat more expensive, will restore your home to its previous condition, using materials and workmanship of similar quality.

For an additional premium, you can also

protect covered personal property on a replacement cost basis (the cost to buy a new identical item today), without incurring a loss because the items have depreciated in value over time.

Earthquake and flood insurance:

These coverages are provided through a separate policy. The federal government is the ultimate guarantor for flood policies.

Umbrella liability:

This vitally important policy provides excess or catastrophic protection to the basic liability protection offered with most other P&C policies. The liability coverage offered by an "umbrella" policy begins where the coverage in a basic policy leaves off, and may actually offer broader protection. If you incur a legal obligation to a third party due to your negligence, this form of insurance covers your financial exposure. You could incur liability as a driver of an automobile, as a homeowner or through professional negligence. Standard policies specifically exclude liability arising from a number of activities or situations, which limits the insurance company's exposure and allows the insurer to provide the protection most commonly needed at a reasonable cost. You can elect to cover these excluded risks by paying an additional premium to purchase an "endorsement." If an endorsement is not available, you may have to purchase a separate policy.

You need to understand the insurance contract.

As an insured individual, you should read and understand key policy provisions of the contract between you and the insurance company. These include:

• *The "perils" (risks) covered in the policy.* In the "named-peril" form, the policy specifies only those perils that are covered. In the "all-risk" form the policy lists only those perils that are not covered, and provides protection for all others.

• *The perils that are not covered.* By securing an endorsement and paying an additional premium, you can usually cover perils that are excluded in the standard contract.

• *The policy limit.* This limit is the maximum benefit or coverage that the insurance company will pay in the event of a loss. You should make sure that the policy will reimburse you for the current replacement cost of the insured item.

- ***The deductible.*** A "deductible" refers to the part of the loss the policy buyer must pay before the insurance company pays its portion. It represents the self-insurance element in an insurance policy. The deductible can be a stated amount or a percentage of the insured value at the time of a loss.

More about liability limits and deductibles.

In standard homeowner's or automobile insurance policies, the deductible amount is usually $250, $500 or $1,000. In theory, if not in practice, the company will reimburse you up to the value of your loss after you satisfy the deductible. For example, if you have a $250 deductible and suffer a car accident with a repair bill of $800, you must pay the first $250. The company should then pay the remainder of $550.

Low deductibles can be a source of waste and inefficiency in your financial economy. For example, if your auto policy has a $250 deductible and you incur a repair bill of, say, $500, would you put in a claim or just pay the entire bill? Most people will think twice about putting in a claim they can afford to pay, because their insurance company will consider the claim when calculating future premiums. If you would pay a repair bill larger than your deductible, the extra premium you are paying for your smaller deductible is a source of financial waste. Raising your deductible to the amount you can comfortably pay out of pocket will lower your premium.

You may also benefit by increasing the liability limits on your auto and home policies. Low liability limits protect insurance companies, who are most concerned with limiting their ultimate liability. Make sure that your policies are designed to serve your needs, not those of the insurance company.

Replacing your earning potential for your family.

Here is why you should be concerned about the limits of your personal liability. Suppose you have a car accident, and you are responsible for the death of another individual. The victim's family would probably sue you and if you were judged responsible for the accident, they would win. How much money would they sue you for? Their attorney would compute the victim's future earning potential. This is a present value calculation of future earnings, usually increased by a projected inflation rate. The calculation may include the value of benefits such as health insurance the victim was receiving, and an amount for pain and suffering.[2]

Suppose you had fatally injured a 40-year-old married individual who was earning $75,000, and who intended to work until age 65. Twenty-five years of lost earnings amount to nearly $2,000,000. The family may also lose other economic benefits the victim was receiving, such as medical insurance. How would you pay the judgment? Your automobile insurance would pay up to its limit (usually $100,000 for an individual and $300,000 for additional passengers), and you and your family would be responsible for paying the balance. You could lose your savings, your home and part of your future earnings.

The personal liability umbrella policy protects you from financial ruin. The policy supplements your home and auto insurance, and can be purchased in units of $1,000,000. Umbrella coverage is inexpensive compared to the level of protection it provides. To obtain coverage you frequently must undergo some underwriting (examination of your driving record and prior claims) by the insurance company. If you qualify you may be offered

The personal liability policy protects you from financial ruin.

several million dollars of protection at a cost of a few hundred dollars per million. Consider purchasing the *largest* personal liability umbrella policy you can secure.

Your property/casualty broker can also help you acquire additional insurance to protect you against hurricane or wind damage, the theft of your personal articles and collectibles, and other coverage that may be relevant in your particular circumstances. Ask your broker to explain how your current policies work and in what circumstances they *do not* protect you. This field is very complex and you need to find a competent professional to help you minimize the risk of losing all you own.

Disability income protection insurance.

Let us say that you are offered the use of a printing press that produces dollar bills each time you turn a crank. You are permitted to turn this crank each year until the machine produces your annual salary. You are responsible for maintaining and insuring the machine. How much insurance would you buy? Most of us would agree that we would attempt to purchase the maximum coverage we could obtain.

You are, in effect, just such a machine. Each day that you are able to get up and go to work, you will earn your salary. But if you cannot work, your income stops. In fact, your ability to work may be your greatest financial asset! Disability income insurance is an essential component of your plan. If you are unable to work, it will replace a portion of your income for a specified period. Policies offer a variety of features, benefits and conditions. You must pass both financial and medical underwriting requirements for this coverage. Most policies offer a choice of monthly benefit amount (up to approximately 2/3 of your income), duration of benefits (up to a lifetime benefit period), a cost-of-living increase option, a future increase option, and partial or residual disability benefits. Some polices offer "own occupation" income protection, which means that if you cannot work in your specific occupation but could work in another capacity, you would receive benefits. In some policies, benefits are "integrated" with Social Security disability payments, which means that your payment will be reduced by the amount you receive from Social Security.

Your ability to work may be your greatest financial asset.

Many public educators are partially insured against a loss of income due to illness or accident. In New York, for example, the pension system provides a member under age 55 with a disability benefit of at least 1/3 of final average salary (usually the average of the last three years' earnings). However, if you qualify for the disability benefit, you do not get a pension. The disability income benefit provided by the pension system is always much less than the member's annual income. Because the member pays no premium for the coverage, the disability payments are taxable when received. It is prudent to purchase a private disability income policy to make up for the shortfall. After all, if your employer told you that your future earnings were going to be only one-third to one-half of your present salary, would you look for another job? Do not put yourself in that situation if you become disabled. In some states, educator associations offer members inexpensive disability income policies. Before purchasing a policy, make sure you fully understand how you could qualify for benefits, and what limitations the policy imposes on these benefits.

As with all insurance policies, you have to pay the premiums. Disability income protection insurance premiums can be higher than you anticipate. You may be tempted to take your chances, rather than spend a few thousand dollars a year for this protection. Consider this: If you were offered a choice of two jobs, which would you take? The first pays a salary of $60,000 as long as you are able to work, and nothing if you become disabled. The second pays a salary of $57,000 but if you cannot work, you will receive a tax-free salary of $40,000 until age 65. Most of us would choose the latter job offer. In this example, the $3,000 salary difference represents the annual premium for a disability income policy (the actual premium depends on your specific circumstances). Is the assurance that your income will continue if you are disabled worth the cost of the coverage?*

> * Disability insurance premiums depend on your age, occupation, and the benefits and policy riders you select. The younger you are when you purchase the policy, the lower the premiums will be.

Good disability income insurance is not cheap. You may have to spend from one to two percent of your annual salary to purchase an adequate policy. As an employed educator, you are the goose that lays golden eggs. Do not merely insure the eggs: protect the goose's ability to lay the eggs!

Good disability income insurance is not cheap.

What happens to your family's lifestyle if you die tomorrow?

Life insurance, one of the nation's oldest and best financial products, is the financial instrument most people choose to protect others in the event of their death. Insurance policies are either permanent or remain in force for a stated "term."*

*Term insurance becomes expensive at higher ages, and has no buildup of cash values. It provides a death benefit for a given period of time. Premiums may be level for a set period (5, 10 and 15 year periods are common) or may increase each year (yearly renewable term). At older ages term premiums become very costly.

Your planner can help you calculate how much capital your family will require if one or both spouses die. Life insurance is designed to provide this needed capital. Most financial planners assume that if one spouse dies, the family requires only 70% of the income to maintain the needs of the remaining family members. Ask yourself whether your car insurance protects only 70% of the car's value, or whether you home insurance covers only 70% of your home's replacement cost. Why would you value your life any less than you do your car or home? Life insurance should provide a *complete* replacement of the lost item or income. Make sure that your planner knows your feelings in this regard. You may want your survivors to have the same income or even more than you now earn, in the event of your death.

Unfortunately, many people use cost as a basis for deciding how much life insurance to purchase. Your planner should be able to show you how to insure your full human life value at minimum cost.

Suppose you are the sole breadwinner in your family. If you have minor children, in the event of your death, the last thing you may want is for your spouse to be forced to find a job. If a parent dies, the surviving spouse needs to comfort and care for the children, and should not be concerned with replacing the deceased's income. And if your spouse currently works, would you not want him or her to spend more time with your children if you are no longer around?

Permanent life insurance can be a flexible product. Besides providing an income tax-free death benefit in most circumstances, permanent life insurance makes it possible to create tax-favored wealth while you are alive. It enables you to fully utilize other assets throughout your retirement, with the comfort of knowing that assets you have consumed will be replaced at your death with an income tax-free death benefit. Cash value life insurance allows you to access funds through policy loans. These loans will reduce your cash value and death benefit.

Life insurance is a legal contract between a policyholder and an insurance company. The company promises to pay a specified sum of money to the designated beneficiary upon the death of the insured individual. Every policy has an owner, an insured individual and one or more beneficiaries. One or more individuals, a business entity or a trust may own the policy. Similarly, the beneficiary may be one or more individuals, a business entity or a trust. The insured individual may own the policy.

The policyholder agrees to pay a stipulated premium for the future insurance benefit. The policyholder can also be the beneficiary. The policyholder may change the beneficiary at will, cancel the contract, withdraw cash values, etc.

Make sure you understand the provisions, guarantees and risks within each life insurance contract you are considering. Insurance companies operate in an environment of increasing disclosure. The Commissioner of Insurance closely regulates the practices of the thousands of companies licensed to do business in each state. No matter where you live, do not rely solely on a state insurance department to protect your rights. You have to educate yourself about the particular contract you intend to purchase.

Qualifying for private insurance: the underwriting process.

The process by which an insurance company decides whether to offer a policy to an individual is called "underwriting." The company requires that the individual seeking insurance fully disclose his or her health history by accurately answering all of the questions on the application.

The proposed insured is usually required to undergo a physical examination by a paramedic or physician and must furnish proof of financial ability to pay the premiums. The applicant's age and the desired amount of insurance determine the scope of the exam. The exam may include only detailed medical history, blood pressure and HIV tests. A paramedic conducts this exam, usually at the applicant's home or place of business. If the applicant is older and is applying for a large death benefit, he or she may have to undergo a full exam by a physician, usually including an EKG, and in some cases even a stress test. The applicant pays nothing for these medical tests. The company determines financial suitability by an examination of financial data, and may also examine the applicant's credit history, driving record, and his or her participation in such activities as scuba diving, piloting a plane, and mountain climbing.

The company may offer the individual a non-standard policy with higher than normal premium if the individual's medical records and exam results indicate less than good health. In some cases the policy may have a temporary substandard rating for a period of years, the premium then reverting to standard level. Or the company may decline to issue a policy. In certain cases, insurance companies spread their risk by the process called "reinsuring," which means that more than one company assumes the risk.

What kind of life insurance should I purchase?

Only permanent life insurance will provide lifetime protection for the policy beneficiary. The most popular types of permanent life insurance presently being marketed are *whole life, universal life, variable life* and *variable universal life*. These differ in structure, guarantees and flexibility of premiums and investment choices.

Only permanent life insurance will provide lifetime protection for the policy beneficiary.

The components of a permanent life insurance policy.

Figure 1 illustrates how the death benefit, the amount at risk and the cash value of any permanent life insurance policy are related to one another.

When the policy begins, the insurer bears the entire death benefit risk. As time goes on, the cash value of the policy grows. At all times the insurer is at risk for the difference between the cash surrender value and the death benefit.

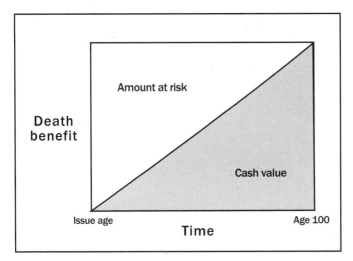

Figure 1: Relationship between the components of a permanent life insurance policy

Whole life insurance.

A company that sells whole life insurance invests the premiums paid by policy owners in its general account and makes certain guarantees to the policy owners. If the policy owner pays premiums, the company will guarantee a death benefit and a cash value, as well as interest, expense and mortality charges. State insurance agencies oversee companies to make sure these guarantees are met.

Over time, the policy builds cash value that the policyholder may draw upon. The company guarantees a minimum interest rate on cash values, usually on the order of 4%. The cash reserves are available under certain conditions to the policyholder during the insured's lifetime. This "cash value" build-up is free of current income taxes, and may be withdrawn as a loan. Policy loans will reduce the cash value and death benefit.

The company may experience a surplus in a particular year. The surplus is divided among the policyholders on a *pro rata* basis and is credited in the form of a *dividend* to each owner's account. Dividends are considered to be a return of premiums paid, as long as they do not exceed the policyholder's basis (the sum of premiums paid into the policy). The policyholder may withdraw dividends up to his or her basis without incurring taxation. Although companies that sell whole life insurance illustrate dividends, they clearly state that future dividends are not guaranteed.

The policyholder may withdraw dividends up to his or her basis without incurring taxation.

The policy is structured so that the cash value equals the death benefit at age 100, when the policy is said to "endow."

Universal life insurance.

Universal life policies offer variable premiums and death benefits. Unlike whole life, the mortality charges within universal life may vary from current to guaranteed levels. The insurance company guarantees a minimum interest rate on cash values, on the order of 4%. Illustrations provided by agents to prospective policyholders show the impact on both cash values and death benefits of paying a given premium for a certain number of years, at both current and guaranteed rates and expenses. Like whole life contracts, universal life's cash value is invested in the general account of the issuing company.

Universal life policies are more flexible than whole life policies in that the policyholder may, after the first year, vary the size and frequency of premium payments. They are also much more sensitive to interest rate changes than whole life policies.

The owner can choose to add the cash value to the death benefit. In that case, the amount at risk (the death benefit which the company must pay at the insured's death) stays level, instead of decreasing each year by virtue of the cash value increase.

Variable whole life insurance.

Variable whole life has fixed premiums and a minimum guaranteed death benefit. In these respects it is more like traditional whole life than universal life. It is also a security, and a prospectus must accompany any offer of sale. A portion of the premium is used to pay the cost of insurance. The policyholder instructs the company to invest the remainder (if any) into one or more segregated funding options. These sub-accounts usually include one or more stock funds, bond funds and a money market fund. Because the policyholder chooses among the available funds, whose performance is not guaranteed, there is no minimum guaranteed cash value in variable whole life policies. Although the cash value may drop to any value, if premiums are paid the death benefit will not fall below the original level. Conversely, if the performance of the funding options exceeds expectations, both the policy cash value and the death benefit may rise. If the funding options include equities, which have over the long-term outperformed inflation, variable life policies may provide a measure of protection against loss of purchasing power. Over the short term, however, policyholders may experience fluctuations in cash value. Thus, variable life insurance may be suitable for people with a tolerance for fluctuations in market performance who wish to combine insurance and potential protection against inflation in one financial vehicle.

Variable universal life insurance.

Variable universal life is an insurance contract with death benefits, policy values and other features traditionally associated with life insurance. A hybrid of universal life and variable life, it is also a security, and a prospectus must accompany any offer of sale. The policyholder assumes the investment risk in this type of life insurance.

The policy is "variable" in that the cash value will increase or decrease depending on the performance of the funding options or sub-accounts. These are assets segregated from the issuing company's other assets, and divided among separate sub-accounts. Advisors hired by the company manage the sub-accounts. The policyholder directs the company to use excess premium payments (premiums less cost of insurance and other policy fees and charges) to purchase shares of one or more sub-accounts.

Most variable universal policies offer a wide range of funding options, spanning several popular asset classes. Variable universal insurance policies may be attractive to individuals who wish to choose to invest the excess premium in specific sub-accounts offered within the insurance contract, thus creating their own portfolio. In a whole life policy or universal life policy the insurance company selects the underlying funding choices.

The policy is termed a "flexible premium" contract because, unlike traditional insurance policies, there is no fixed schedule for premium payments. The policyholder may vary the frequency and amount of future premium payments subject to certain limits, restrictions and conditions set by the issuing company and by federal tax laws.

How much life insurance is sufficient to replace my income?

At the insured individual's death, if the policy is in force, the company will normally pay the net death benefit to the policy beneficiary.*

* This assumes that the policyholder met company requirements. If the policy is still within the contestability period (usually two years from the date of issue), and the insured committed suicide or made a material misstatement on the application, the company may not be required to pay the net death benefit.

Suppose the beneficiary chooses to invest the proceeds in an interest-bearing account and withdraw only the interest as it is earned. Here is a useful rule of thumb: every $100,000 of life insurance death benefit, if invested prudently to produce interest of 5%-6% (assuming such an account is available at that time), should produce $5,000 to $6,000 of annual taxable income for a survivor. Therefore, if you want your survivor to have an annual income of $50,000 to $60,000 in the event of your death, and he or she can find a stable interest-bearing account that produces 5% to 6% annual interest, your survivor will need $1,000,000 of capital to generate this income. You may also want to provide your survivor with enough money to pay for college, to pay off a mortgage, and so on.

Long-term care insurance.

Like most people anticipating retirement, you may be planning for travel, recreation and an independent lifestyle. You are counting on your pension, Social Security and the pool of assets you have painstakingly accumulated during your working years. But a serious long-term illness or accident could drastically change your lifestyle. Ask yourself these questions:

What would happen to my family if either my spouse or I required three years of long-term care, costing potentially as much as $300,000? What impact would this have on our lifestyle, our retire-ment plans, our savings account and our ability to help our children? What would be the impact on our estate?

Long-term care is the help you would need if you could not take care of yourself for an extended period of time. It refers to the kind of care or help that you may need for conditions related to the natural aging process, or to an accident, disability, chronic illness or a cognitive impairment such as Alzheimer's Disease.

Long-term care includes custodial care that may or may not follow a medical event. We need long-term care when we have a physical impairment or cognitive disorder that requires the services of others. For example, a person who develops severe arthritis may be unable to perform normal activities without assistance. We may lose the capacity to bathe, dress or feed ourselves, transfer from a bed to a chair, remain continent or use the toilet. Or we may develop senile dementia or Alzheimer's Disease. Our ability to conduct the activities of daily living, as well as maintain our mental acuity, determines whether we would qualify for long-term care benefits under federal programs such as Medicaid and Medicare.

Do not think of long-term care as being just for the elderly. It is true that more than half of the people who need long-term care today are 65 years old or older. But 40% of the people who need this care are between the ages of 18 and 64. The number of individuals with severe disabilities between the ages of 17 and 44 has increased fourfold in the past twenty-five years.[3] An individual could experience an automobile accident, a heart attack, a stroke or other incapacitating events at any age, and thereafter require long-term care.

The chance of needing long-term care is much greater than most people anticipate. Most people insure their homes and personal property against fire and theft damage. No matter how unlikely our chance of using this coverage, we maintain our homeowner's insurance year after year because the probability of a loss is small but not zero. We protect ourselves against the risk of being sued in an automobile accident and our automobiles against damage or theft, even though we may consider ourselves to be careful drivers who are unlikely to need this insurance.

More than 60% of all Americans will need long-term care at some point in their lives.[4] The majority of those who need long-term care (about 57% of the population) are over age 65. The need for care increases with age. If you are between ages 50-65, you have a 10% chance of needing long-term care. From age 65 to age 80 the probability increases to 25%, and reaches 50% above age 80.[5] But nursing home costs are just a small fraction of the total long-term care problem in America. For every person in a nursing facility, there are many others receiving similar care at home or in the community. In 1997, four out of five people who took on the role of primary caregiver to the disabled elderly were family members.[6]

How much does this care cost?

In 2002, a day of skilled/intermediate long-term care in a nursing home varied widely with location. It ranged from $90 in Louisiana to $280 in New York City to $410 in Alaska.[7] The cost was highest in the northeastern U.S.[8] Home healthcare can cost more or less than confined care, depending on the level of care. Custodial care is relatively inexpensive, but skilled care may cost more than $50 per hour in some locations.

How people pay for long-term care:

- By using their income or savings.[9]

- By relying on Medicare or Medicaid. However, as we will see, Medicare does not really cover the costs and Medicaid requires the applicant to impoverish him or herself to qualify for benefits.

- By purchasing a long-term care insurance policy, which is frequently the best and least expensive way to pay for this care.

Federal and state programs for long-term care.

Why do we need private long-term care insurance? Because despite what you may have heard or now believe, the government will probably not pay for our long-term care costs. Americans today live significantly longer than they did as recently as 1970, when our average life expectancy was 70.8 years. By 1998 this average was 76.7 years, an increase of 8.3%, and the Census Bureau projects life expectancy to rise to 78.5 years in 2010.[10] According to the Healthcare Financing Administration, federal, state and local governments pay for about 23% of the cost of home healthcare, and about 35% of nursing home costs.[11] Individuals and families pay approximately 43% of home healthcare and nursing home costs. The result: In 1998 more than 70% of single individuals who required long-term care, and 50% of couples with one partner in a nursing home, were impoverished within one year.[12]

As we have seen, the older we become the greater the chance of our needing long-term care in a nursing home, our own home or in an adult day care facility. Since 52% of people age 65 or over can expect to require some long-term care during their lifetime, two-thirds of all couples will need long-term care for at least one spouse. Unfortunately, unless you are impoverished and have "spent down" much of your personal savings and other available resources — including private insurance — the government expects you to pay for your care.

Many of us erroneously believe that Medicare and Medicaid will cover us in the event of a long-term care confinement, but this is not the case. Medicaid is a very complex program and can be difficult for even the experts to understand. Medicare has limited long-term care benefits and Medicaid will only pay for care for the impoverished. See Appendix B for an explanation of how Medicaid and Medicare operate.

Long-term care insurance: a solution

Long-term care insurance is relatively new. Although policies have been available for about 15 years, a few companies made serious marketing efforts in the late 1980's. In the last ten years, there have been many "generations" of such policies, with a liberalization of benefit triggers and a proliferation of new policy benefits.[*]

* Most policies reimburse policyholders for incurred expenses. Some companies offer an indemnity contract that pays the daily benefit regardless of the expense incurred.

Features and benefits of policies:

Today, the typical policy may offer these features and benefits:

- Nursing home care daily benefits ranging from $40 to $250.

- Benefit duration ranging from 2 years to lifetime.

- Three levels of care covered: skilled, intermediate, and custodial.

- Care provided in the community is covered, such as an assisted living facility and adult day care center.

- Home and community based healthcare benefits ranging from 50% to 100% of the nursing home daily benefit.[13]

- Waiver of the premium for home care and nursing home care after the elimination period has been satisfied, or when benefits commence (criteria vary significantly among companies).

- Extended grace period for payment of premium due to cognitive impairment.

- Choice of elimination or waiting period for benefits to begin, ranging from zero days to 360 days. In some cases, the elimination period only has to be satisfied once in a lifetime.

- Benefit triggers that may include cognitive impairment [14] or the inability to perform at least two of the six "activities of daily living"[15] without substantial assistance.[16]

- Choice of no inflation, 5% simple or 5% compound inflation of daily benefit.

- Care coordinator benefit: a licensed case management agency assesses the insured individual's need for long-term care, creates and implements a plan of care and periodically reviews progress.

- Alternate plan of care coverage provides services required to enable the patient to live as independently as possible.

- Modification of the home for the benefit of the individual under care (wheelchair access, for example), and emergency medical response systems.[17]

- Bed reservation benefit: pays to reserve bed or room in a facility while the patient is hospitalized. This permits the patient to return to the chosen facility.

- Choice of licensed or non-licensed caregiver.

- Informal caregiver training.

- Respite care, providing temporary relief for the primary non-licensed caregiver (usually a family member); the maximum amount covered is usually a multiple (20- 30 times) of the daily benefit.

- Spousal and preferred rate discounts.

- State-qualified policies that protect assets.

- New tax-qualified policies allow the policy-holder to take a federal tax deduction as medical expense for a portion of the premium.[18] Any policy sold before 1/1/97 is considered tax-qualified.

- A non-forfeiture benefit, under which the insured has an amount of paid-up insurance either at a reduced benefit or for a limited time.

- Benefit payments generally coordinated with Medicare payments, so that the insured individual does not receive both benefits simultaneously.

Qualifying for long-term care insurance.

As with life insurance, an applicant for long-term care insurance must complete a detailed questionnaire and undergo medical and financial underwriting to qualify for a long-term care policy. The questionnaire focuses on medical history and the applicant's ability to perform the tasks of daily life without assistance. If the applicant states that he or she needs help with the activities of daily living or has a cognitive impairment, the application is generally rejected. For example, an applicant with severe arthritis who uses a walker will be rejected at the application level. The applicant must also permit the company to investigate his or her medical records. Unlike the life insurance underwriting process, long-term care underwriting procedures rarely require the younger applicant to undergo a physical exam. Beyond a threshold age, a paramedical exam (blood pressure and HIV testing) may be required. Some applicants may

The applicant must also permit the company to investigate his or her medical records.

also have to pass a cognitive awareness test, conducted face-to-face or by telephone interview.*

* Companies keep the contents of such tests confidential. However, they may require the applicant to listen to and recite from memory a list of numbers and names.

The underwriting process may take a few weeks to several months. At the time of application, the applicant may "bind" the application by tendering part of the annual premium when completing the application. The company investigates the applicant's medical history, and will offer policies to those applicants who meet the underwriting standards (usually health and financial) of the issuing company. For example, if an applicant is unable or needs assistance to perform the defined activities of daily living, (eating, bathing, transferring from a bed to a chair, toileting, continence and dressing), or has been diagnosed with a cognitive impairment, the company will usually reject the application. Many companies issue standard, preferred and "rated" policies, depending on the health of the applicant. Rated policies carry extra premiums to offset the extra risk the company assumes. A rating may increase the premium and/or limit the policy benefits. If the application is rejected, or if the applicant chooses not to accept the policy within a 30-day "free look" period of time, the company will return any premium tendered with the application. However, if the application is bound with a deposit, the applicant may have temporary coverage.

How benefits are triggered.

For benefits to be received under a tax-qualified policy, the insured individual is assessed by a licensed healthcare practitioner and deemed to need at least 90 days of care for an "activity of daily living"-type impairment. The 90-day certification requirement does not apply to a cognitive disorder. In general, the individual who requires care has either lost the ability to perform two of the six activities of daily living, or has developed a cognitive disorder. Qualified long-term care services are defined under IRS Sec. 7702B(c)(1) as "necessary diagnostic, preventive, therapeutic, curing, treating, mitigating, and rehabilitative services, and maintenance or personal care services, which" are required by a chronically ill individual and are provided under a plan of care prepared by a licensed healthcare practitioner. Benefits begin under a policy when covered qualified long-term care services have been received, in accordance with the individualized plan of care, and after the elimination period has been satisfied. Benefits you receive from a tax-qualified policy are generally tax-free. Under indemnity policies in which the per diem benefit is paid regardless of cost incurred, the company may pay the claimant a higher benefit than the cost the claimant incurred. In this case, to the extent that the excess benefit exceeds $220 in 2003, only the excess is taxable.[*]

[*] For example, if the daily benefit is $250, and the claimant spends $50 on care, he or she may keep the extra $200 without incurring income tax. However, if the claimant spent only $25 on care and received $250 from the insurance company, the extra $25 would be taxable.

Long-term care premiums.

The level annual premium for a long-term care policy varies from company to company, although the premiums fall into a narrow range. The premium is affected by the choice of benefits: the daily nursing home benefit; the home healthcare benefit; the benefit duration; the elimination period and the inflation option. A spousal discount and a discount for "preferred" status will lower the premium.

The premiums for a long-term care policy are guaranteed renewable for the life of the policyholder. Although no individual policyholder can be singled out for a rate increase, the company may apply for a rate increase (or decrease) by "class." If the state commissioner of insurance approves the rate change, the new premium must apply to the entire population or "class" of policyholders (i.e., all Nevada residents). Companies hope to avoid increasing premiums on in-force policies, but from time to time, it occurs. Thus, policyholders have no guarantee that the premium stated in the policy will persist throughout the life of the policy-holder. As policyholders grow older and utilize their coverage, companies may deem it necessary to raise premiums on existing policies in order to maintain profitability.

Deductibility of premiums for long-term care.

Section 213 of the Internal Revenue Code permits individuals to deduct qualified long-term care premiums and unreimbursed medical expenses for those taxpayers who itemize. Figure 2 illustrates the maximum tax deduction for qualified long-term care premiums based on attained age before the close of the reported tax year.

Attained age before close of year	Maximum premium deduction per individual
40 or less	$250
Between 41 and 50	$470
Between 51 and 60	$940
Between 61 and 70	$2510
Over age 70	$3130

Figure 2: Maximum tax deduction for qualified long-term care premiums at various ages.

Suppose a 62-year old individual purchases a long-term care policy with an annual premium of $3,000, and has other unreimbursed medical expenses of $4,000. If this individual's adjusted gross income was $50,000, he or she meets the 7.5% threshold for medical deductions, since 7.5% of $50,000 is $3,750 and the total unreimbursed medical and premium expense is $7,000. The medical expense deduction would be $3,250 ($7,000 minus $3,750).

Comparing policy features, cost, availability and suitability.

The National Association of Insurance Commissioners has developed worksheets[19] to help consumers gather and evaluate information about the cost and availability of long-term care; the benefits of various policies; whether purchasing a policy is the best option; and if so, which policy would best meet the specific needs of the individual. A qualified insurance agent or financial planner can help you obtain the data necessary for a thorough analysis. You may also contact your state insurance department or agency on aging for assistance with questions about Elder Law and long-term care.

Of the many risks in retirement, the financial risk associated with needing ongoing care is perhaps the most overlooked. Yet, it is statistically likely that you or your spouse will need this care. The purchase of long-term care insurance is by far the most cost-effective method of protecting your assets.

Long-term care insurance should play a major role in your risk management plan, once you reach your fifties. A long-term care event could have a devastating impact on your lifestyle, your retirement plans, your savings, and your estate. The annual premium will probably be only 1%-2% of your net worth, yet in the event you need this care the insurance will protect your entire estate. Your planner should help you find premium dollars to pay long-term care insurance premiums. Secure this essential insurance once you reach age 50, or earlier if you can afford the premium. There is no guarantee that you or your spouse will be healthy enough to qualify for coverage at a later age.

HOW YOUR PENSION REALLY WORKS

As you approach retirement, you will probably schedule a pension consultation with a counselor from your retirement system. For many educators, this consultation is the first opportunity they will have to learn how their pension really works, and how in some ways it actually works against them.

The retirement benefit programs and the rules that govern them vary widely across the nation. Some state teachers retirement systems require member contributions. Some retirement systems increase benefits annually by means of a cost-of-living adjustment (COLA); others do not. Some systems permit retirees to alter their initial beneficiary choices in case they divorce. Some systems integrate retirees' pensions with Social Security benefits, reducing the burden on those states to provide pension benefits. Some permit retirees to accelerate Social Security payments in their early retirement years, reducing their pensions in later years. (See Appendix C for an overview of Social Security benefits.) You should contact your state teachers retirement system at least a year before you plan to retire, in order to become familiar with the array of choices open to you.*

* Visit your state teachers retirement system's website for a detailed description of how your pension is calculated, and what survivorship option choices are available to retiring educators in your state.

Let us listen to a hypothetical conversation between John, a 55 year-old high school math teacher, his 55 year-old wife Molly, and a Teachers Retirement System counselor. After a discussion of how John's pension will be calculated, John expresses his desire to have his pension payments continue if he predeceases Molly. He has heard that it is possible to provide for a survivor by choosing among a variety of "options," but he does not understand how they work.

JOHN: "First off, I want to understand how the state will calculate my pension. Can you tell me how they do it?"

COUNSELOR: "John, our state uses a formula method for calculating your pension.[20] The retirement system's computer programs will arrive at your maximum pension based on your years of service and your final average salary. In your situation, you are credited with 2% of your final average salary for each year of service. If you did not have sufficient service years or retired before the required age, you would lose some pension benefits. But I see that you will have 30 years at retirement, and will be 55 years old, so you meet the state's criteria for full retirement benefits. In that case, you will have a maximum possible pension of 60%."

JOHN: "What do you mean by maximum possible pension?"

COUNSELOR: "Well, John, without getting too technical, I can tell you that your pension as calculated by the formula is really a single life annuity. This means that as long as you live, you will receive a monthly benefit check. But I assume that there is someone in your life that you love more than our pension system. Am I correct?"

JOHN: "Of course! I am looking at her right now. What happens when I die? Can I pass my pension on to Molly?"

COUNSELOR: "Yes, you can. But in that case, you will not get your maximum pension. The state will take back a portion of each pension payment, because you elected to protect a beneficiary."

JOHN: "I do not like the idea of losing part of my pension, but I suppose nothing is free in this world. Molly must be protected if I die first. Tell me about our options. What choices do we have?"

COUNSELOR: "Well, John, your Teachers Retirement System gives you a number of ways to protect Molly in case you die first. You can select either a joint and survivor option or a period certain option. Let us look at the period certain options first. These options guarantee payments for certain periods of time. By the way, how is your health?"

JOHN: "I am fine...at least that is what my doctor says. Why do you ask?"

COUNSELOR: "Because period certain options assure that you will receive your pension as long as you live, but if you die within the stated period, your beneficiary or beneficiaries will continue to receive income until the end of the period. One option runs for 5 years and another for 10 years. If you chose the first option and lived more than five years, your beneficiaries would get nothing. However, if you died in the second year, they would continue to receive income for three more years. The same would apply to the ten-year-certain option. That is why I asked if you were healthy. Most healthy retirees will not risk leaving their beneficiaries with no income if they outlive the period of the option. By the way, these options are not free gifts: you will lose part of your pension if you choose one."

JOHN: "What other choices do I have?"

COUNSELOR: "The joint and survivor options may work better for you both. Under the 100% option you will get a monthly income smaller than you would have if you selected taking your maximum pension. When you die, Molly would continue to get the same monthly income for the rest of her life. That is what the term "100%" refers to: Molly gets 100% of your reduced pension benefit at your death. You could also choose a "50%" or "25%" pension for Molly, but they may not give her enough income to live comfortably after your death."

MOLLY: "What happens when *I* die? Can I pass the income to the kids?"

COUNSELOR: "Sorry. You cannot. The pension payments will end at Molly's death."

MOLLY: "Wait a minute. John will have worked for thirty years when he retires. Are you saying that all that effort is lost when we are both dead? We can't pass on anything from his pension to our children?"

COUNSELOR: "Molly, I do not make the rules. But if it makes you feel better, every educator in the country shares this problem with the two of you."

JOHN: "What if Molly dies first?"

COUNSELOR: "You will continue to receive your reduced monthly income the rest of your life. Some state retirement systems, such as Wisconsin's, permit the retiree to choose another beneficiary if the original survivor dies or changes marital status (such as divorce). Unfortunately, in our state, New York, you cannot select another beneficiary to receive your pension if Molly predeceases you."

MOLLY: "John, I am *thankful* that we live in a state where I will not lose your pension if we get divorced. After all, we have been married for thirty-five years and I earned the right to receive your pension if you die first."

JOHN: "Do not worry, darling. We have a really solid marriage and you do not have to worry. But I can't believe that the state will keep taking money out of my pension check even though no one will benefit when I die."

COUNSELOR: "There *is* a way around this problem. Another option called a "pop-up" allows you to revert to your maximum pension if Molly predeceases you. But I have to warn you: this option is even more expensive than the regular joint and survivor option."

JOHN: "I understand that it costs me more because I am getting more protection, but by how much will this reduce my pension each year?"

COUNSELOR: "I will calculate that for you in a few moments. It ranges from a few percent to nearly 25%, depending on your relative ages. I will put a printout in the mail this afternoon, once I calculate your numbers. Before we end our meeting, do either of you have any other questions about the pension options?"

MOLLY: "I do. You haven't mentioned what happens if I die and John chose a survivor-ship option. Will he be able to transfer his pension to others, such as our children or his next wife?"

JOHN: "No one can replace you, darling, but that is a good question. Can I pick another beneficiary if my circumstances change?"

COUNSELOR: "No, you cannot. In fact, if you divorce and remarry, Molly will continue to be your beneficiary under your pension, even if you all agree that your new wife needs the protection more than Molly." *

* This is not the case in all states. For example, retired Connecticut and Wisconsin (among others) educators who divorce may select their new spouse as beneficiary. The option costs for their new situation are computed at that time.

JOHN: "Can't we pass on the pension to our children?"

COUNSELOR: "California allows you to name multiple beneficiaries, but this is not the norm across the country. In New York, the only way to leave John's pension to a child is for you to name a child as a beneficiary from the start. Notice that I said '*a* child.' If you have two or more children, you can choose only one as your survivor. In terms of your pension benefit, you have to disinherit the others. And since a child has a long anticipated lifetime, it costs the retiree more to select a child as survivor. In some cases, choosing a much younger person as survivor really reduces a pension, perhaps by as much as 30-40%!"

John and Molly left this meeting enlightened but disappointed with the choices they have to make when John retires. They felt that their pension system penalized retiring educators with dependents who want to protect their loved ones after their death. And even if they lived to a ripe old age, John and Molly were concerned that their children will not benefit from John's pension, under any circumstances. This conversation with a retirement system counselor, repeated thousands of times each year across the country, contains all of the information most pre-retirees will receive before they make an irrevocable and costly decision. However, there are other ways for a retiring educator to protect not just his or her primary beneficiary, but also the entire family, in case of the retiree's death.

Pension basics.

No matter where you work, when you retire from public education your pension benefit depends on a number of factors:

• Your age at retirement. You are penalized if you have worked the appropriate number of years but choose to retire before you reach the age for full retirement benefits.

• Your credited years of service. What constitutes service credit, and the rules for purchase of prior or out-of-state service, vary from state to state. If you decide to retire before completing the necessary years of service you may have to accept a reduction in pension benefits.

• Your final average salary or your three highest annual salaries.

• Your own contributions to your retirement, if any. Some states match employee contributions.

• The "tier" to which you belong. Many state teacher retirement systems are organized on a "tier" system, the earlier tiers generally affording better benefits.

• The per year percentage applicable in your tier. This varies from state to state, averaging between 2% and 2.5% per year for older teachers with extended service. Many states have established a maximum percentage (75% of final average salary in New York), no matter how many years the educator has worked.

• Whether you want your pension to continue for a survivor at your death.

• If you have accumulated funds in a tax-sheltered annuity (403(b) plan), whether you annuitize the account at retirement or delay withdrawals to a later date.

Every state offers numerous options, both *period certain* and *joint and survivor*, for passing part of a pension to a named beneficiary. Every option reduces the retiree's pension benefit.

Most state retirement systems use a variant of this formula:

Single life annuity=years of service x final salary x per year percentage

The factors described above, i.e., choice of survivorship option, early retirement reduction etc. may reduce the maximum pension. In certain states, members are required to participate in creating their retirement fund. The Connecticut Teachers Retirement System requires all members to contribute 7% of their annual salaries on a pre-tax basis.* New Jersey educators must also contribute to their retirement funds. In all states, retirement benefits depend on the member's age, years of service, final average salary (average of your three highest paid years) and the retirement formula for which the member qualifies.

* A portion (1%) of your contribution goes to defray the health insurance costs for retired members and spouses.

Pension options.

A retiring member of every state teacher retirement system must choose from among several pension benefit payout options. Choices include *maximum pension (single life annuity), a period certain option* or a *survivorship option (joint and survivor annuity).*[*] Some states also offer retirees a *declining-reserve* option and a *partial-refund option.* You elect the option at the time of retirement, and in many states your choice is irrevocable.

[*] In Connecticut, the survivorship option is called "co-participant option."

Consequences of taking maximum pension.

Your maximum pension allowance is in essence an immediate *single life annuity,*[**] which means that you will receive a check from your pension system, no matter how long you live. If you choose a maximum pension, your pension payments will cease at your death. No payments will continue to your survivor or heirs.

[**] A single life annuity is an income stream that will continue for the lifetime of the annuitant. An immediate single life annuity, as the name implies, begins when the contract is purchased.

However, if there is someone who depends on your pension for support, you may want to make another choice: a *period certain* or a *joint and survivor* option. Therefore, most retirees will not select the single life annuity (maximum allowance) without taking steps to provide ongoing income for their survivor, since their pension will stop when they die. Because no one knows how long he or she will live, electing the maximum pension allowance exposes your beneficiary to the risk that you will die prematurely. In that case, your pension could stop long before the death of your survivor.

If you choose a maximum pension, your pension payments will cease at your death.

If there is **anyone** in your life whom you love more than your teachers retirement system, taking the maximum allowance without using other planning options can cause those individuals to suffer financial hardship when you die.

Incidentally, "anyone" can include a relative, friend, charitable institution or university.

Period certain and survivorship options: passing your pension on after your death.

Joint and survivor options let you spread your pension over two lifetimes. With a period certain option, when the retiree dies, the named beneficiaries continue to receive income until the end of the stated period. Under a joint and survivor option, when the retiree dies the named beneficiary or survivor continues to receive income throughout the survivor's lifetime. With either type of option, there is an ongoing cost.

When you elect an option, you agree to surrender a portion of your pension each year to provide for your survivor's income.

When you elect an option, you agree to surrender a portion of your pension each year to provide for your survivor's income.

Period Certain or Guarantee Options.

Period certain or guarantee options provide a benefit for a survivor if the retiree dies within the term specified. In many states, retiring members may choose a guarantee period of 5, 10, 15, 20 or 25 years.

With a period certain or guarantee option, the income will continue to the end of the stated term and then cease. For example, if a member selects a 5-year period option and lives only three years, the named beneficiary will receive the same allowance for two more years. If the retiree lives beyond the guarantee period, no benefit is paid to the survivor. Selecting these options will cause a reduction in the pension paid to the retiree.

To summarize, period certain options assure that you will receive your pension as long as you live, but if you die before the end of the stated period, your beneficiary or beneficiaries will continue to receive income until the end of the period.

Declining Reserve Option.

Many states also offer members a *declining reserve* option. For an annual reduction in pension benefits, the retiree secures the right to pass on the unused portion of his or her pension reserve account to a named beneficiary or beneficiaries. Each year the reserve is diminished by the payout to the retiree, who may elect calculations at different percentage rates. The lower rate gives the retiree a smaller pension but preserves more of the reserve. The higher rate election does the opposite.

This option may be of interest to retirees who enter retirement with low life expectancy, because the shorter their life span, the more money will pass to their beneficiaries. On the other hand, if the cumulative pension payments equal or exceed the initial reserve amount, at the retiree's death the beneficiary will receive nothing. If this point is passed while the retiree is still living, pension benefits continue for the life of the retiree.

Joint and Survivor Options.

Joint and survivor options (also called survivorship options) do not have a time limit beyond which income ceases. The retiree selects the beneficiary at the time of retirement. The choice of beneficiary is usually irrevocable during retirement and only one can be named. Some states restrict this choice to a family member; other states permit the selection of an irrevocable trust with a single beneficiary.

To calculate the cost of a joint and survivor option, your pension system utilizes actuarial tables that specify the probable life expectancy of two individuals, the retiring member and the named beneficiary or survivor. The annual reduction in the retiree's pension depends on their relative ages at the time of retirement. The smaller the age difference between the retiree and named beneficiary, the lower the "option cost" or reduction in pension. If the named survivor is much younger than the retiree, the annual cost of the survivorship option will be greater than if they were of equal age. If the retiree is much older than the named beneficiary, the option cost can become a sizable fraction of the maximum allowance.

However, if the survivor is much older than the retiree, the annual cost to insure the pension for the survivor will be smaller than if they were the same age. Many states have adopted unisex actuarial tables that replaced the gender-based tables previously employed to calculate survivorship option costs. Calculations based on the new tables frequently result in lower option costs.

Think of the annual option cost as an insurance premium that the retiree pays each year to the retirement system. The option cost guarantees an annuity payment to a survivor upon the retiree's death. As we will see, this method of creating a potential income stream to a named beneficiary may be expensive and restrictive when compared to other strategies, but it is available to all retirees within the system.

For a given retiree and survivor, the option cost also depends on whether the retiree chooses to leave the same pension benefit (100% option), one-half the benefit or a smaller benefit to the named beneficiary.

What happens if the survivor predeceases the retiree?

In some states, if the survivor predeceases the retiree, under the normal survivorship options the retiree continues to receive the same reduced pension allowance as when the survivor was alive. The retiree *may not be permitted to assign the survivor's benefit to another individual.* Thus, the guaranteed annual loss of pension — the option cost — continues until the retiree's death.[21] A second type of joint and survivor option called the "pop-up" remedies this defect. If a pop-up is elected, and the named beneficiary dies before the retiree, the retiree reverts or "pops up" to the maximum allowance.

The retiree may not be permitted to assign the survivor's benefit to another individual.

Some states require retirees to specifically elect a pop-up option; in other states the "pop-up" is built into the option. In those states, if the survivor predeceases (or, as in Connecticut, becomes divorced from) the retiree, the retiree automatically pops up to maximum benefit. "Pop-up" options cost more than the regular joint and survivor options, because they indemnify the retiree against a continuing annual option cost in the event of the premature death of the survivor.

Reviewing the rules controlling joint and survivor pension options.

If you select maximum pension, all payments stop at your death. Therefore, if there is *anyone* you love more than your state teachers' retirement system, without taking additional steps to protect your survivor, you cannot risk taking maximum pension.

If you select a maximum pension, all payments stop at your death.

If you select a period certain option, you will receive a reduced pension for the rest of your life. If you outlive the stated period (i.e. 5, 10, or 20 years) and then die, your named beneficiaries receive nothing. If you die within the stated period, your beneficiaries continue to receive payments until the end of the period.

The reduction in your pension for any option depends on the relative ages of the retiree and survivor. The younger the named beneficiary, the greater the annual reduction in allowance.

Some states allow educators to choose a declining reserve option, which passes whatever remains of the pension reserve to named beneficiaries upon the death of the retiree.

Under a joint and survivor option, you receive a reduced pension throughout your lifetime. If you predecease your survivor, he or she will continue to receive payments for their remaining lifetime. All payments stop at the death of the survivor.

The reduction in your pension is a guaranteed annual loss that continues each year throughout your retirement. It is an insurance premium paid to your retirement system each and every year of your retirement, which can amount to a significant fraction of your pension allowance.

Under a "pop-up" option, which is automatic in some states, if the survivor dies first, the retiree reverts to maximum pension. Pop-up options cost more than simple joint and survivor options.

Under a joint and survivor option, once a survivor is named, that choice is irrevocable in many states after you retire. (Some states, such as Idaho, permit a change of option if you were single when you retired, and you marry in retirement. Wisconsin allows a new choice of survivor after a divorce).

If you elect an option, and your pension system has an automatic cost of living increase (COLA), you lose the COLA on the option cost. This compounds the reduction in later years.

You can only choose one beneficiary under a survivorship option; if you have two or more beneficiaries, you must "disinherit" all but one.

Survivorship option costs for John and Molly.

Let us revisit John and Molly, who just received the printout of John's retirement benefits and option costs. John is now age 55 and ready to retire. Molly is also age 55. John will retire with 30 years of service. In his state, his maximum pension is based on a "final average salary (FAS)" calculation that uses his three highest paid years. His FAS will be $60,000. His retirement system credits him with 2% of FAS for each year of service. Therefore, his maximum allowance will be 60% of FAS or $36,000.

Let us assume John is a member of a typical teachers retirement system. The 100% option choice, as a 55 year-old retiring educator with a 55 year-old named survivor, reduces his maximum pension by about 10% a year, or $3,600. John would receive $32,400 during his lifetime, and at his death Molly would receive the same annual benefit throughout her remaining lifetime. If John predeceases Molly, all payments will stop at Molly's death.

If Molly were younger than John, the option cost would be higher. The reduction in *maximum pension is approximately 1% for every two years of age difference. Thus, if Molly were 47 when John retired at age 55, the 100% option would cost them 14% of John's pension or $5,400 a year.*

What is John's lifetime cost of selecting an option? At age 55 John has a 27-year life expectancy. At an assumed net 6% cost of money (the hypothetical rate we assume John could earn on annual deposits of his option cost), $3,600 a year would grow to $243,100. At a net 8% cost of money, the option losses accumulate to $365,651. Clearly, the lifetime cost of selecting a survivorship option is significant for many families.

What happens if John waits five years to retire? They will both be age 60 at that point. Assuming the same final average salary of $60,000, here is the table of the survivorship option choices available to John and Molly.[22]

Pension options	Annual benefit	Reduction
Single life annuity	$36,000	$0
100% joint and survivor	$31,565	$4,435
75% joint and survivor	$32,573	$3,247
25% joint and survivor	$33,617	$2,383
5 year certain	$35,812	$188
15 year certain	$34,373	$1,627
100% survivor, 15 year certain	$34,121	$4,579

Figure 3: Joint and survivor options for John and Molly retiring at age 60.

Figure 3 illustrates the cost of various survivorship options for John and Molly. Suppose John selects the 100% survivorship when he retires at age 60. At retirement, he would receive $31,565 each year. He would then pay the retirement system $4,435 a year for this option. If he predeceases Molly, she would continue to receive $31,565 each year. At her death all pension payments would cease. However, if Molly died first, John would continue to receive the reduced allowance of $31,565. Although he continues to pay the annual option cost, John is prohibited from naming another beneficiary.

How permanent life insurance can replace a survivorship option.

Because the pension stops at the retiree's death, a retiree who wishes to leave part of his or her pension to a beneficiary should not select maximum pension.

Is the joint and survivor option the only other choice? As we have seen, when a retiree elects a joint and survivor option to protect a beneficiary, the pension system takes a portion of the retirement allowance each year. This portion of the pension is similar to an insurance premium that the retiree pays to the pension system each and every year in retirement. The "insurance" benefit from the pension system comes in the form of an income stream that ends at the death of the survivor. Unlike a private life insurance policy, there is no lump sum death benefit that accrues to the family of the retiree. The retiree has no access to the annual option payments. Once

Is the joint and survivor option the only other choice?

retired, the retiree cannot rescind his or her choice of option, nor can he or she change the beneficiary. Few people with other choices available would buy such a restrictive insurance policy from a private insurer.

The joint and survivor option is available to every retiree, regardless of his or her health. Private insurers will not insure every applicant. To qualify, one must meet the insurer's underwriting criteria, including health and financial stability. Thus, not every retiring educator can obtain private life insurance. All educators will qualify automatically for a joint and survivor option. Under what conditions does private life insurance provide better benefits than joint and survivor options from the pension system?

Not every retiring educator can obtain private life insurance.

How life insurance can preserve your pension for your survivor.

When one analyzes the problem of protecting a survivor in retirement, it comes down to this: the survivor needs to have enough money at work to produce a livable income. With sufficient capital invested, after your death your survivor will not need your pension payments. The survivor can create an income stream equal to the survivorship option pension by investing the pool of capital. Where will this pool of money come from when the retiree dies?

Permanent life insurance can create the required pool of capital just when it is needed: at the death of the retiree. The survivor can then create his or her own pension, by either prudently investing capital and living off the income or by purchasing a single life annuity, thereby creating a guaranteed lifelong income. If the survivor wishes to live off the income rather than purchase an annuity, the more money the survivor invests, the lower the required rate of interest he or she must earn to produce the same annual income stream.

Permanent life insurance can create the required pool of capital just when it is needed.

If the survivor has a large enough pool of money to invest at the death of retiree, he or she can even "inflation-proof" his or her future income by taking more money over time as inflation reduces purchasing power. If the survivor does not consume all of the capital, what remains at death can be passed on to children or grandchildren. Life insurance has few of the restrictions inherent in every joint and survivor option the pension system offers.

If the retiree can qualify for and afford to purchase a permanent life insurance policy, the policy may be a useful product for pension protection for these reasons:

- The retiree's death creates an income tax free death benefit.

- The retiree and spouse may choose the death benefit to replicate or even exceed the reduced pension allowance available under a joint and survivor option.

- If the retiree is disabled and cannot pay premiums, under a disability waiver of premium rider the company will pay the premiums. Definition of disability and age restrictions apply to this feature.

- Policy cash values are available through low interest policy loans. These loans will reduce cash value and death benefit.

- The portion invested grows tax-deferred.

- The policyholder can name multiple beneficiaries and change them at will.

- The policyholder can terminate the policy if it is no longer needed, recovering the surrender value.

- The death benefit, if not fully depleted at the survivor's death, can be passed to other heirs.

- Under certain conditions,* premium payments may cease during the life of the retiree, in effect restoring the maximum retirement allowance.

* Life insurance companies do not guarantee that policyholders will be able to stop paying premiums at some point in the future, although this can in fact occur.

How much insurance do I need to replace my pension for my survivors?

There are two methods of calculating the life insurance death benefit required to replace the equivalent joint and survivor option benefit: *the annuity method* and the *interest-only* method.

The annuity method computes a lump sum that, if annuitized by the survivor following the death of the retiree on the day of retirement, would provide a life income to the survivor equal to a particular joint and survivor option allowance. Using John and Molly as an example, the lump sum death benefit required to replace John's "full" allowance is $534,000[23]. If John died the day after retiring, Molly could annuitize this sum and receive a lifetime income equivalent to the pop-up option allowance. Annuity payments are larger if one purchases the annuity at an older age. Therefore, the longer John lives in retirement, the larger Molly's annuity income would be, since she would purchase the annuity at an older age. Furthermore, Molly may elect to take a joint and survivor annuity, naming a child as the survivor. This could enable her to pass a portion of the proceeds to the next generation, which is not possible under state retirement system joint and survivor rules. This choice would, however, require that Molly accept a lower annual payment than if she had chosen a single life annuity.

The interest-only method provides income for the survivor based on a reasonable, attainable rate of return. This method assumes that the survivor will invest the insurance proceeds in a financial instrument that yields a stable interest rate. If the retiree wishes to replace the joint and survivor option allowance for a beneficiary, one could calculate the necessary interest rate based on a given death benefit. In selecting an instrument, it is wise to be conservative. One should plan for a yield that has been historically achievable, keeping in mind that past performance does not accurately predict future behavior of equity markets.

Figure 4 illustrates average annual compound returns of various asset classes over the period from 1/1/70 to 12/31/99. The average annual return depends on the timing and frequency of investments. This table[24] assumes a single investment in 1970 with reinvestment of dividends and interest.

Asset Category	Before inflation	After inflation
Stocks	13.7%	8.2%
Bonds	9.2%	3.9%
Cash equivalents	6.7%	1.5%
Cash under a rock	0.0%	- 5.1%

Figure 4: Returns from various asset categories from 1/1/1970 to 12/31/1999

In our example[25], if we choose a taxable non-inflation-adjusted yield of 4%, a lump sum death benefit of $789,000 invested at 4% would produce interest income equivalent to that of the full survivorship option.[26] At John's death, Molly receives the insurance proceeds free of federal or state income taxes. At that point she has many options:

- She can invest the death benefit and withdraw only the interest income, if sufficient, thus preserving the principal for her children.

- She can invade the principal and increase her annual income.

- She can buy an annuity and create a guaranteed lifetime income. She can choose a time when interest rates are high to maximize her lifetime income. The older she is when she annuitizes, the larger her income will be.

- She may annuitize the money over two lifetimes, in effect choosing a joint and survivor option at a later date. This option reduces her income but enables her to pass income to another beneficiary at her death.

How can you determine if life insurance is a better choice for your situation than a pension option?

Compare the life insurance premium to the option cost.

If the life insurance premium is approximately the same as the net-after-tax survivorship option cost, the pre-retiree should strongly consider the life insurance alternative. First you must determine your annual pension reduction if you select a particular survivorship option.[27] Then you must estimate the after-tax cost of the survivorship option.[*] Compare the after-tax cost of the survivorship option with the annual premium for a life insurance policy of sufficient death benefit to produce the desired pension for your survivor.

* The option cost reduces your pension and therefore, reduces federal income taxes. The "net cost" of the option is the reduction minus the taxes you would have paid on this income.

If he can secure coverage for an annual premium that is comparable to the survivorship option, this may be a better choice.

What if private insurance is more expensive than the option cost?

In this case, you must consider other factors. These include:

The possibility of premium offset.

It is important to keep in mind that the survivorship option loss is an ongoing annual cost to the retiree. The retiree will pay this cost each year until his or her death.* In contrast, it may not be necessary to pay the annual premium for a permanent life insurance policy for the rest of one's life. Under certain (non-guaranteed) circumstances, the policy-holder may be able to cease paying premiums at a point in the future, because the company may be able to withdraw future premiums from dividends and cash value. Insurers will project this "offset point" for a proposed insured, under various scenarios of premiums and rates of return. If the premium does offset, the retiree in effect "pops up" to maximum pension while still protecting the beneficiary. The possibility of the cessation of premium payments, while not

* Unless the retiree chose a "pop-up" option and the beneficiary pre-deceases the retiree.

guaranteed, may be a factor in determining whether to select a survivorship option or private insurance.

The "legacy" factor

Under the survivorship option all payments stop at the second death. With private insurance, it is possible that a portion of the insurance proceeds will pass to the heirs after the death of the retiree or survivor. If the survivor predeceases the retiree, who maintains the insurance coverage, the heirs will receive the death benefit. If the retiree predeceases the beneficiary, he or she may not consume the entire death benefit.

Change of marital status

In some states, if the retiree elects a survivorship option and divorces during retirement, the original beneficiary designation stands. Private life insurance is more flexible, permitting the policyholder to change the beneficiary and add others.

Protecting multiple beneficiaries

In the majority of states, you can select only one beneficiary to receive your pension benefit upon your death. A life insurance policy may have several beneficiaries, and the policyholder may change these designations at will.

Access to policy cash values, if any, during retirement

The policyholder may withdraw cash values at will, subject only to contract provisions. However, it usually takes many years for significant cash values to build within most policies, and the contract imposes surrender charges on withdrawals during the early years. Because permanent life insurance contracts may[28] develop cash values, they can serve as one among other financial instruments that accumulate and afford access to money. If the retiree survives the beneficiary and the insurance protection is no longer required, the retiree may terminate the policy and withdraw the cash surrender value. Any gain (surrender value less cumulative premiums paid) would then be taxable. Alternatively, the retiree may borrow a portion of the surrender value, which will reduce the surrender value and the death benefit.

What kind of life insurance should you purchase?

Only permanent life insurance will provide a lifetime protection for the survivor.[29] The most popular types of permanent life insurance presently being marketed are *whole life, universal life, variable life,* and *variable universal life.* These differ in structure, guarantees and flexibility of premiums and investment choices. See chapter 2 for details on each type of policy.

When should you purchase life insurance for pension protection?

In general, purchase as much as you can afford of the necessary insurance as soon as you can. Ideally, by the time you retire you should have sufficient permanent life insurance in place to protect your pension. The younger you are, the smaller the annual insurance premiums you will pay. Further, if you have purchased a whole life policy, which earned dividends over the years, it is possible that the death benefit will increase over time, providing more protection for the survivor the older you become. If you delay purchasing insurance and your health deteriorates, you may be forced to select a survivorship option.

As previously discussed, under certain conditions you may be able to cease premium payments at some point during your ownership of the insurance contract. If this occurs by the time of retirement, you will not have to apply a portion of your pension for insurance premiums. When you start your retirement, you will truly be at "maximum pension."

How do you select the right insurance company?

If you express interest in purchasing life insurance, your planner will contact insurers and secure policy illustrations for you to examine. Companies such as A.M. Best, Moody's, Fitch, Inc., Standard & Poor's and Weiss Research, Inc.[30] rate insurers and publish their findings. This information is available from many sources, including the companies themselves. Not every company is licensed to sell all types of insurance. If you are planning to purchase a variable policy, make sure that the companies you investigate offer this equity-based product.

How will you pay the premiums in retirement?

If your planner has done a good job, you will have recaptured money that was leaking out of your financial life. This wasted money may come from term insurance premiums you no longer have to pay, because you now have permanent insurance coverage. You may have refinanced your home and paid off other non-tax-deductible debts, freeing money each month for premium payments. You may have begun to make systematic withdrawals from non-sheltered investment accounts to pay premiums, thereby avoiding an increasing future tax burden as the accounts grow over time. You may pay part or all of the premiums with the portion of your pension you would have paid to your state teachers retirement system for a survivorship option.

It is possible that after many years, cash values within the policy could "offset" or pay future life insurance premiums. If your planner shows you an "offset" illustration, keep in mind that these projections are not guaranteed, and that you may have to pay premiums throughout your retirement. However, if the contract actually does offset, allowing you to cease paying the premium, you would in effect "pop up" to maximum pension. Of course, the required rate of return or dividends must continue at the "offset" level for the rest of the contract, or premiums would resume. If you have purchased a whole life policy that pays a dividend, you may be able to use dividends to reduce the premium. Keep in mind that dividends are not guaranteed, and you may have to pay a larger portion of the premium in a given year if the dividend is smaller than projected.

Should you plan to use the cash value as a retirement supplement?

The cash value in a permanent life insurance policy is a financial asset that policyholders can use under certain conditions. In my opinion, however, you should not count on using this asset to supplement your retirement income.

Permanent life insurance policies may accrue cash values over time. In whole life policies, guaranteed cash values build up over the years. The company may also declare dividends, which add to the policy values. Variable contracts are more directly subject to market fluctuations than whole life policies, and their cash values are not guaranteed and will tend to fluctuate more than whole life contracts.

Only a portion of the accumulated cash value is available to the policyholder in the early years. The insurance company imposes a decreasing surrender charge on withdrawals in the first several (perhaps as many as 15) years. If the policyholder terminates the contract, he or she may incur a surrender charge. This charge vanishes over many years, so if the policyholder surrenders the policy in later years, the surrender charge may be slight or even zero. When cash does become available, the policyholder may surrender his or her basis (the cumulative premiums paid into the contract) without taxation, or borrow from the surrender value. The policyholder may also surrender without taxation, up to basis, the cash value of any additional insurance (called "paid-up additions") purchased with policy dividends that may have accumulated in the contract. Policy loans taken from the guaranteed cash value are also tax-free.[31] Both surrenders and policy loans will decrease cash values and death benefits. Although cash values in excess of basis may be borrowed without taxation, if the policy lapses or is surrendered, any gains withdrawn become taxable to the policyholder.

Policy loans taken from the guaranteed cash value are also tax-free.

As we have seen, the cash value within a permanent life insurance policy is an asset and may under certain conditions be withdrawn to supplement the retiree's income. If you are planning to use the cash value, make sure you examine illustrations that show the effect on death benefit and potential future premium payments. Think carefully before borrowing cash values for non-essential reasons, because you may end up canceling the policy in the future when both loan interest and additional premiums are due.

How time may enhance the survivor's pension.

Previously we calculated the required life insurance death benefit by computing the cost of an annuity that would replicate the survivorship option pension. In this calculation, we assumed that the retiree would die on the first day of retirement. However, as the beneficiary grows older, the same death benefit used to purchase an annuity will produce a larger income for the survivor, who has a shorter life expectancy at that point. If the retiree and survivor do not anticipate needing a larger annuity payment for the survivor, because they can draw on other assets to compensate for inflation, they could decide to reduce the death benefit at an older age. One way to accomplish this is to borrow some of the cash surrender value. Another way is to request that the insurer reduce the death benefit, if the contract permits this.

Who should own the life insurance contract?

Although the beneficiary of a life insurance policy receives the death benefit free of federal, state or local income taxes, the proceeds are included in the policyholder's estate. This could have a substantial impact on estate taxation. Therefore, who owns the policy must be considered in formulating an estate plan. This is discussed at length in chapter 5.

Purchasing life insurance inside your 403(b) tax sheltered annuity plan.

Tax sheltered annuity contribution rules

Your tax sheltered annuity plan (also known as a 403(b) plan) is funded by salary deferrals. For 2003, the Internal Revenue Code generally limits TSA salary reduction contributions to 16-2/3% of gross income up to an annual maximum of $12,000. In special cases, this limit may be exceeded. For example, if you have been in service in the same district for more than 13 years but only recently began a TSA, you may catch up by contributing up to $13,000 for a specified number of years. There is an exception to this limit: if an educator has 15 or more years of service with the same employer, an extra $3,000 may be deferred provided that no more than an additional $15,000 is contributed in a lifetime. Further, the average yearly contribution may not exceed $5,000.

An educator may also make a "year of separation" election.[32] For tax years beginning in 2002 and later, the 16-2/3% limit is eliminated. The deferral limit is $12,000 in 2003, increasing by $1,000 each year thereafter until it reaches $15,000 in 2006 and later. It is further adjusted for inflation in $500 increments after 2006. Excludible contributions are limited to 100% of compensation. Individuals who have reached age 50 can make an additional "catch-up" contribution of $1,000 in 2002, increasing by $1,000 each year thereafter until reaching $5,000 in 2006 to 2010. Beginning in 2011, the provisions applicable in 2001 are scheduled to become applicable again when the 2001 Tax Act "sunsets."

IRS rules for purchasing life insurance in a TSA

The IRS allows you to purchase "incidental" life insurance within your TSA, using pre-tax dollars. The word "incidental" means that the government limits your premiums to just under 50% of your total TSA contributions (past, present, and future) for whole life policies, and up to 25% of your contributions for universal or variable universal life. You may transfer[33] up to 25% of your existing total contributions into a variable or universal life policy or up to 50% into a whole life policy, without causing a taxable event. You may also direct a portion of future TSA payroll deductions to pay for your policy. Because the insurance policy is part of your tax-sheltered annuity program, your access to the cash value within your TSA life policy will be subject to the same IRS restrictions as your TSA accounts.

Keep in mind that allocating a portion of your TSA contribution to life insurance will result in a smaller TSA balance than if your entire contribution were invested, since part of your contribution will pay the cost of insurance.

Paying the premium with salary deferral dollars may be a tax-efficient way to purchase life insurance. You save taxes on the premiums, because the contribution decreases your gross income. For example, if you are in a 28% tax bracket, you need to earn about $139 for every $100 you spend on life insurance outside a TSA plan. Therefore, the after-tax cost of life insurance is much lower if purchased inside a TSA.

For example, if you are in a 30% tax bracket and your life insurance premium is $2,500, you would have to earn $2,500 divided by 0.7, or $3,571, to net the same premium after taxes. By allocating $2,500 of your TSA contributions to a life policy, you reduce your taxes by $2,500 times 30% or $750.

Tax treatment of TSA life policies

When you own a life insurance policy within your TSA, you have to report a small amount of the premium as taxable income each year, an amount equal to the cost of term insurance coverage. Each year, you will incur income taxes on either the actual mortality expenses (insurance charges) for your policy, or on what the Internal Revenue Service calculates the insurance is worth, taken directly from IRS "economic benefit" tables, whichever is lower. The "economic benefit" varies by age and the amount of protection. In practice, this usually amounts to less than $100 of income tax, so there is considerable savings by purchasing the insurance inside a qualified pension plan. For example, a 35-year-old educator with $100,000 of insurance protection would include $57 in gross income for that tax year.[34] Assuming a 28% tax bracket, this would result in a tax of less than $16.

As with ordinary life insurance plans, cash values within the policy grow tax-deferred. And if the insured dies before retiring, the beneficiary receives the death benefit. The amount of the proceeds equal to the cash surrender value, minus the accumulated economic benefit costs that were included in the deceased participant's income, is taxable. The remainder is free of income tax.

Removal of the insurance from the TSA at retirement

The laws governing life insurance contracts held inside a 403(b) plan (TSA) require you to remove the insurance contract from your TSA at the time of retirement. You can accomplish this in various ways, each with its own tax ramifications:

1. You may surrender the insurance and transfer the cash value, if any, into your tax-sheltered annuity. The value of your annuity will increase by your life insurance policy's cash surrender amount. Your life insurance protection will no longer remain in effect. There will be no current taxes triggered by this transaction. However, you have eliminated the possibility of using the insurance to provide a survivor's pension.

2. You may transfer the life insurance out of your tax-sheltered annuity and continue the policy separate from the plan. Your life insurance protection will remain in effect. The cash value of your policy will no longer be subject to the IRS restrictions imposed on your TSA plan. In the year you retire, you will pay current income taxes on the difference between your policy surrender value and the total mortality charges or economic benefit cost for which you already paid taxes.

3. If you cannot afford to purchase your policy, you can have the trustees of your

TSA take a loan against the policy cash value and then transfer the policy ownership to you. There should be no taxable consequences to this transfer, as your policy will have only a limited amount of cash value on the transfer date. At the close of the transaction, your policy will have a loan with loan interest that will be added to the premium each year. The policy death benefit will be reduced by the outstanding loan. The pension benefit will not be included in your income until it is actually received.

To summarize, as with any planning strategy, there are advantages and drawbacks to TSA life insurance. It may be an appropriate choice when an educator needs life insurance protection while in service, and can use pre-tax dollars to purchase permanent coverage without stressing the family budget. This coverage can later serve to protect the educator's pension for a beneficiary. However, it is unlikely that a policy purchased within a TSA will suffice for complete pension protection, because of the IRS limitations on the premium. Because the policy must separate from the TSA at retirement, in most cases the policyholder will experience a taxable event. You can minimize the tax by controlling how much cash value you retain within the policy, and how much you transfer back into the TSA.

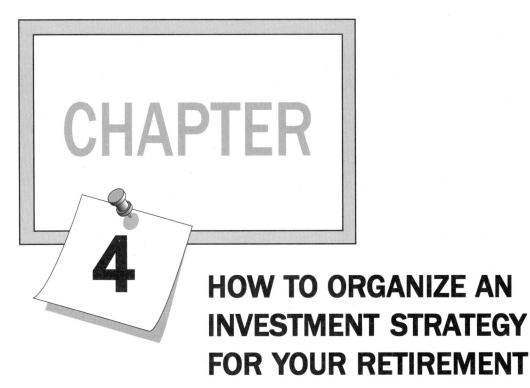

CHAPTER

4

HOW TO ORGANIZE AN INVESTMENT STRATEGY FOR YOUR RETIREMENT

If you would like to someday retire with a smile on your face, you have to pay more attention to retirement funding than people generally did thirty years ago. Educators who retired in 1970 at age 65 had a 6-year life expectancy. By 1998 the average life expectancy of a retiree increased to 76.7 years, so that a 65-year-old retiree could look forward to an average of 12 years in retirement. The average life expectancy is projected to reach 78.5 by 2010.[35] If you are in the early years of your career and are

If you are in the early years of your career and are planning to retire at age 55, your money may have to last for decades.

planning to retire at age 55, your money may have to last for decades.

While you are employed you would be wise to try to save and invest as much money as you can for your retirement years. You must also develop a strategy for drawing upon your savings and investments during your retirement. It is important to focus on both processes because the strategies used to accumulate wealth differ from those used to distribute this wealth during retirement.

Why you may need to plan for an ever-increasing family income.

Inflation has been a constant feature of our economic system. It will probably continue throughout our lifetimes. Let us take a closer look at the history of inflation in the last twenty years from the perspective of a consumer. Suppose in 1980 you lived in an urban household and spent $100 on goods and services as defined by the consumer price index (CPI-U).[36] In 1985 you would have needed $131 to purchase the same goods and services. By 1990 you would have needed $159. In 2000, you would have had to spend $209 to purchase goods and services that $100 would have bought you in 1980. Many fixed-income retirees are deeply concerned about this 200% increase in the cost of goods and services. No one can predict the future course of inflation, but it is prudent to take this economic factor into account when creating your financial strategy for retirement.

I began teaching in 1970 at Mamaroneck High School in Westchester County, NY, with a starting salary of $13,000. I retired twenty years later while earning $55,000. My raises averaged a respectable 6%. However, our family did not experience a measurable increase in our purchasing power as a result of my nearly four-fold increase in salary. My family's personal rate of inflation, which was affected by large increases in our property and school taxes, to name just one factor, far exceeded the national averages during those years. Despite my sizable raises, which compared well with those that many of my friends in private industry received, we fell behind in purchasing power. For example, in the last years of my teaching career we had to send our three kids to college. As a result, we found it much more difficult to make ends meet on my final salary than on my much smaller 1970 salary. Because of inflation, our purchasing power had lost ground each year. From many conversations over the years with fellow educators, I am convinced that my family's experience with shrinking purchasing power was typical in the New York educator community.

Let us analyze how a typical educator family may cope with the problem of retiring in an inflationary environment. Larry, a teacher in a middle school, is about to retire at age 62. He and his wife Marge wish to maintain their present lifestyle, which requires $60,000 in today's dollars. Larry's pension and Social Security will equal Larry's present salary. They are concerned about whether their income will keep pace with inflation as they grow older.

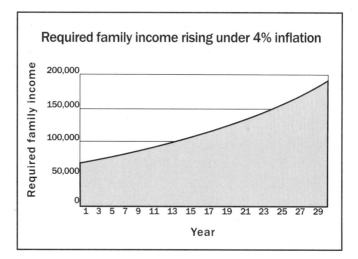

Figure 5: Increasing income required to maintain purchasing power under 4% inflation.

Figure 5 illustrates how Larry and Marge's income must increase to keep pace with inflation. Let us assume that inflation will reach 4% each year during the next thirty years, well below the past 25-year average. In that case, Larry and Marge will require an ever-increasing income to maintain their standard of living. Their 2001 annual income of $60,000 must increase to *$187,000* by 2031 for them to maintain purchasing power. * Suppose that Larry's state teachers retirement system applies a cost-of-living adjustment (COLA) equal to the CPI inflation rate to retirees' pensions. Further, suppose that the government will continue to increase Social Security benefits to keep pace with the CPI inflation rate. Then their family income will keep pace with inflation. If inflation is their only problem, they may be able to maintain their purchasing power as they grow older.

* This threefold increase in required income may seem an exaggerated projection. However, if you have been teaching twenty or thirty years, think back and compare your starting salary as a teacher to what you are earning today. Did you enjoy a threefold increase in salary, or did your salary increase by a higher multiple?

Other economic forces that affect retirement income

However, Larry and Marge must pay attention to economic forces other than inflation. For their strategy to work as planned, they would have to keep their spending habits constant during retirement, which many retirees find difficult to do. Many retirees discover that filling their free time with meaningful and interesting activities takes more money than they spent while employed. Our technological society continually produces new products and services and renders existing ones obsolete. They may discover that they really need or want to replace old products or services with new and better ones. They may have to dip into their savings to purchase these products or services thereby reducing their capital.

Finally, retirees must recognize that a strategy based on the past behavior of economic variables has no reliable predictive value. No one can guess the future of tax rates, inflation and market performance, all of which will affect purchasing power. If retirees want their strategy to work as planned, they will have to be continually vigilant, carefully monitoring economic indicators and their own propensity to consume.

> No one can guess the future of tax rates, inflation and market performance, all of which will affect purchasing power.

The role your investments will play.

During retirement, as inflation erodes purchasing power, retirees draw from their investments to supplement pensions and Social Security. In our complex economic world, with no certainty as to future rates of return and inflation, you will need to formulate a plan for spending (or spending down) your investments over what may prove to be a very long retirement.

If Larry's pension and Social Security payments do not increase at his family's rate of inflation, the longer he and his wife live the less his pension dollars will purchase. They will have to utilize their savings and investments to supplement their income. Let us consider the extreme case: neither Larry's pension nor his Social Security payments are indexed. If inflation continues, each year Larry and Marge will have to take more money from their investment accounts.

By making a number of assumptions, we can calculate how much money they would need to have invested at the start of their retirement.* Suppose for example that inflation continues at 4%, and that tax rates remain constant. If they earn 7% each year (which no one can guarantee will occur) on their investments, they would need to have $311,000 invested at the start of retirement to provide an annual supplement to their fixed income sources. It is vital that Larry and Marge carefully monitor the performance of their investment

* Keep in mind that for this model to work as planned, Larry and Marge would also have to carefully control spending during retirement, which many retirees find difficult to do.

accounts as they withdraw money each year, because under the above interest rate and inflation assumptions, their money would be exhausted after 30 years. If one or both were still living at age 95, they would have to utilize other assets such as home equity or life insurance cash values to maintain their lifestyle in future years.

Creating an investment strategy.

Your investment strategy in the pre-retirement or savings phase should differ from your post-retirement investment strategy. While working, you should try to save and invest as much money as possible, building the nest egg that will maintain your purchasing power as inflation diminishes the power of your pension and Social Security checks. In this pre-retirement phase, your portfolio should be designed for maximum performance, consistent with your tolerance for fluctuations.

When you retire, you leave the accumulation phase and may begin to utilize your savings to supplement your income. You have entered the spending or consumption phase of your life.

However much capital you have accumulated while employed, you probably will not consume it during the first days or years of retirement. Some planners believe it useful to segregate your savings into different accounts, each intended for use at a specific time. You would then create different investment portfolios for each account. For example, the portion of your capital you need early in retirement in order to supplement your pension and Social Security income would be invested *more* conservatively than money that will be used later on, because this portion *has* to be available when retirement begins. You may invest this "early use" money in a money market or savings account, to avert the risk of even a short-term market downturn.

Conversely, you might invest money earmarked for use many years from the start of retirement more aggressively, on the theory that time will smooth out the fluctuations that aggressive portfolios usually experience. Of course, you must remember that there is *no guarantee* that this will in fact occur, and one is exposed to market risk no matter how long one's time frame.

Besides the possibilities of a long-term market downturn or runaway inflation, you may experience slower financial progress because you may have to pay taxes each year on dividend income and realized gains.* If you hold your

* Realized gains occur when you sell a security for more than you bought it. Gains can either be short-term (you held the security for less than a year) or long term (you held the security for more than a year). The maximum tax rate on net capital gain (net long-term capital gain reduced by any net short-term capital loss) is 15% in 2003. For tax payers in the 10% and 15% tax brackets the maximum tax rate on net capital gain is now 5%.

portfolio within a tax-sheltered annuity or a retirement plan, you will not have to deal with taxation until you begin withdrawing funds, presumably after you retire. At that point you will have to pay ordinary income taxes on withdrawals.*

* Most people who save in qualified plans such as TSAs hope to be in a lower tax bracket when they withdraw their funds than when they made deductible deposits into the qualified plan. It is worth noting that this strategy could fail, either because tax rate could be higher at the time of withdrawals, or because even the minimum required distributions from the qualified plan are large enough to thrust the taxpayer into a higher bracket.

Modern portfolio/ efficient market theory.

In the 1950s, economists developed a theory of investing which attempted to explain how an "efficient market" works. They named their theory *efficient market theory* or *modern portfolio theory*.[37] It has proven useful in the real world of investing.

In an efficient market, all participants have the same information regarding the market as a whole and about specific securities in particular. Even with similar information, participants will value the same securities differently. Buyers of an issue believe the value of the stock is worth more than their money and sellers have the opposite opinion. The securities exchanges, the auction markets that enable people to buy and sell securities, work on this principle. They help buyers and sellers come to a mutually acceptable price for a security. It is statistically unlikely that anyone will outperform market averages consistently. In an age of growing access to information, our national securities markets tend to behave increasingly like efficient markets.

Many small investors believe that skilled professionals with sophisticated securities analyses and timing strategies should be able to consistently "beat the market." The underlying assumption is that markets are inherently inefficient, enabling professionals to uncover specific situations and profit from them. To some extent, this is true. However, most academic and industry research supports the view that markets are, in a broad sense, efficient. The long-term investing techniques presented below conform to the tenets of efficient market theory, and do not depend on timing the market.

How to live with a volatile market.

Although hardly anyone likes the idea that his or her investments will fluctuate, it is part of the investment territory. If you are seeking high returns, you may have to live with more volatility than if your goals are more modest. Every investor reacts uniquely to short-term fluctuations in price. For example, let us say that you can tolerate a 10% decline in your portfolio, but would become so

Every investor reacts uniquely to short-term fluctuations in price.

uncomfortable if it dropped 15% that you would get out of the market. In that case, you should consider investing in a portfolio that is statistically unlikely to vary more than 10% on the downside. Or, you need to learn to look past the short-term fluctuations and remember that markets have performed well over the long term.

Some financial advisors will discover their client's tolerable range of fluctuations or "comfort zone," and design portfolios that historically have fluctuated only within this range. Utilizing this strategy, they hope to keep the client invested in the portfolio over a long time period, even as disturbing short-term fluctuations occur. The advisor has a longer perspective and knows that in the past many asset classes have performed well over the long term. If the client stays invested for the long term and ignores the short-term volatility, he or she should succeed.

How can you learn to live with volatility? *First, invest regularly.* Many people find that automatic investment plans are not only convenient but also provide built-in discipline. You may enroll in your school district's 403(b) tax-sheltered annuity plan and have the business office withdraw and invest your tax-

How can you learn to live with volatility? First, invest regularly.

deferred contributions each paycheck. Or you may start a non-tax-sheltered systematic investment plan with a financial institution. Do not worry about whether the market is up or down on the day you invest each month. The key is to invest regularly and systematically, no matter how the markets perform in a given month. But keep in mind that a regular investment plan does not assure a profit or protect against a loss in declining markets.

Next, buy and hold for the long term. A bull market is a prolonged period in which stock prices generally rise. A bear market is a period of six months or more during which stock prices drop at least 20%. Another bear market starts when the market recovers to the previous high or a year after the market low occurred. Since 1970, there have been approximately equal numbers of bull and bear markets. Bull markets lasted longer than bear markets during this period. The longest bull market (as measured by the Dow Jones Industrial Average) started in 1982 and lasted until the winter of 2000, resulting in a rise of more than 1000%. The longest bear market occurred between January 1973 and December 1974, when the market declined by 45%.

Next, buy and hold for the long term.

Figure 6 shows the history of declines in the Dow Jones Industrial Average since 1900.[38]

Type of decline	Number of declines	Average length	Last occurrence
Moderate (-10% to -15%)	102	113	March 2001
Severe (-15% to -20%)	51	218	March 2001
Bear market (-20% or more)	28	344	March 2001

Figure 6: 100 years of stock market declines

The role of income and dividends.

Your investments can earn income, and that income can also earn income. This compounding effect may have a significant impact on your wealth. If your investments are earning dividends as well as producing income, your portfolio can increase even in a flat market. For example, on November 14, 1972, the unmanaged Dow Jones Industrial Average (DJIA) closed at 1003. On October 12, 1982, after much fluctuation in the intervening ten years, the DJIA closed at 1004. Although the "market" as measured by this index remained essentially flat, a $100,000 investment on November 14, 1972, would have grown to $169,772 by October 12, 1982, thanks to reinvested dividends (not including taxes due during that period).

Is now a good time to invest?

Investing for the long term seems to be a recipe for success. If you attempt to "time the market" and end up buying high and selling low, your portfolio's performance will disappoint you. Staying in for the long run, as we will see, has led to many investors' success since the era of The Depression.

> Investing for the long term seems to be a recipe for success.

No one can accurately predict the future of the equity markets. However, if the market continues to rise, even with intermittent declines, as it has since the 1930s, then waiting for the "right time" becomes costly. Figure 7 shows the results of four hypothetical investors, each of whom invested $10,000 in the S&P 500 Composite Index for the ten-year period that ended on December 31, 2000. Three of these investors moved in and out of the market. The fourth investor stayed invested for the entire ten years, and was much more successful than the other three.[39]

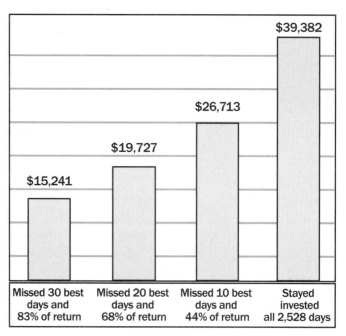

Figure 7: Investing for the short or long term

Once again, however, we must keep in mind that there is no guarantee that the future behavior of markets will duplicate past results.

More lessons from history.

In an information age, anyone who listens to the radio or watches the news hears the daily closing prices of the world's stock markets. Although today's numbers are clearly very important to investors, history can teach us an important lesson about the differences between short-term and long-term performance.

What can we learn from the history of market declines? First, no one can predict consistently when declines will occur. Next, since 1982 declines have been brief, and, for the long-term investor, relatively painless in the long run since the market has always recovered in the past.[40] Finally, it is very difficult for investors to time the market because it requires them to successfully perform two coordinated acts: selecting the right moment to get out and the right moment to get back in. Clearly, *time is the enemy of volatility*. Remember: since the depression era, *the declines have been temporary, the advances permanent*. If you had stayed invested for the long run, you would have had a good chance of succeeding.

Since the depression era, the declines have been temporary, the advances permanent.

Buying during the sale.

There is another way to look at bull and bear markets. In general, as the price of a security increases, its value is gradually extinguished.* A bear market, viewed in this light, can be regarded as a "value rally," because it presents

* Let us say that a security is priced at what is regarded as an appropriate price-to-earnings (PE) ratio for its asset class. If the price increases faster than earnings, the PE ratio increases and the intrinsic value of each share declines.

a short-term opportunity to purchase securities at a relative discount. Of course, it is difficult for many investors to purchase securities in the throes of a bear market. They wonder how long the decline will continue. They ask themselves and their advisors: *Will the market recover? Am I throwing good money after bad?* They express concern that *this* decline is different. But, since 1945, a bull market has overcome and surpassed every bear market, with successive bull markets reaching higher levels than anticipated. As always, keep in mind that past performance does not predict future performance.

A rational investor who intends to keep on investing may ask: *Since I am not finished buying, why would I want the market to continually rise?* And most working educators are not finished buying. They systematically invest paycheck after paycheck, in tax-sheltered annuities and non-sheltered investment vehicles. So when the inevitable downturn occurs, the investor with a long perspective and knowledge of market history will tend to buy or hold, rather than sell.

Dollar Cost Averaging.

Dollar Cost Averaging (DCA) is the process of periodically and automatically investing a fixed number of dollars into an investment. The same number of invested dollars buys more shares at times when the investment is down, and fewer when the investment is up. This technique will generally result in a lower average cost of shares than if the investor bought shares at random intervals. However, in a rising market, Dollar Cost Averaging works against you. In fact, if you expect the investment to increase in value over time, you may be better off purchasing shares all at once, since every share is purchased at the lowest cost.

Dollar Cost Averaging, if done on a payroll deduction or automatic debit basis, helps investors "pay themselves first" by removing the element of decision from the process of investing. For example, if you arrange for a mutual fund company to debit your checking account each month, you will not have that money to spend impulsively. This forced savings aspect of Dollar Cost Averaging may be its greatest benefit because of the way it influences investor behavior. If it is coupled with an automatic monthly withdrawal from, say, a money market account, it creates an automatic savings plan. Remember, a periodic investment plan such as Dollar Cost Averaging does not assure a profit or protect against a loss in declining markets.

The role of diversification in designing your portfolio.

Efficient market theory stresses the overwhelming importance of portfolio design, rather than security selection and market timing, in the long-term performance of a portfolio. The lasting value of this approach is that it enables investors to construct long-range financial plans based on risk-return scenarios that have a statistical likelihood of actually occurring. History has shown that asset class selection had a far greater impact on the success of a portfolio than market timing or stock selection.

The process of combining various asset categories to create a portfolio is termed "asset allocation." It attempts to reduce risk while preserving the possibility of a projected rate of return. An investor employing this strategy combines different types of assets in specific proportions to create a portfolio that reflects his or her tolerance for fluctuations and the desired rate of return. Investors should consider their time horizon for the portfolio, their potential need for liquidity, the tax implications of specific assets, and the potential for changes in economic conditions such as inflation and interest rates. When designing a portfolio, investors can now use statistical data showing the historical performance of certain blends of assets, although it is still important to keep in mind the all-too-true adage that past performance does not predict future results.

Designing portfolios with low volatility.

In theory, a particular asset class responds predictably to a specific economic stimulus, such as a rise in interest rates. For example, if interest rates rise, we expect bond prices to fall. This occurs because the market value of a bond paying, say 5%, must decline if new bonds are available that will produce higher yields. We may also expect stock prices to fall when interest rates rise because of the increased cost of bor-rowing money. The opposite also holds true: falling interest rates usually, but not always, are accompanied by rising bond and stock prices.

As previously discussed, investors become uncomfortable when their portfolios experience fluctuations beyond their comfort zones. Anxious investors tend to sell and lose the advantages of staying invested for the long haul. How might we design a portfolio with reduced volatility? By com-bining asset classes that respond differently to the same stimulus. Certain parts of the portfolio should lag behind others in responding to a change in an economic variable.

How might we design a portfolio with reduced volatility?

We do not want one half of the portfolio to rise while the other half is falling by the same amount: this would cause the portfolio to remain stagnant. But so long as the component asset classes move out of phase with one another, fluctuations in the portfolio may be diminished.

If our portfolio includes diverse asset classes such as foreign securities, domestic and foreign bonds, utility stocks and heath care stocks, economic stimuli will have different impacts on each asset class. Thus, under the influence of a particular economic stimulus, parts of our portfolio will rise and others lag or actually fall. This behavior tends to smooth out the volatility of portfolio values, and may keep us in our comfort zone so that we avoid selling at the wrong time.

For example, stocks and interest-sensitive loans are asset classes that usually respond in opposite directions to a change in interest rates. Imagine an investment comprised of short-term loans to large corporations, where the interest rate charged is the prime rate. Increases in the prime rate will increase the yield of such an investment, and decreases in the prime rate will have the opposite effect. Stocks tend to fall if the prime rate rises, in part because the cost of financing business goes up. If we purchase stock and prime-rate-dependent loans of equal value and the prime rate rises, the value of the stock will tend to shrink and the value of the loans will tend to rise. If the prime rate falls, the opposite tends to occur. Of course, while this strategy reduces fluctuation, it may also result in zero growth. Therefore, in order to reduce volatility but maintain growth potential, a portfolio should encompass a variety of asset classes that move out of phase with one another. Some should rise while others remain stationary, with still other components falling.

A study of how various mixes of asset classes performed, both in volatility and return, over the twenty-year period from 1970-1999, produced some unexpected results.

Figure 8 compares returns from various investment mixes with the volatility that accompanied each mix.[41] A portfolio which consists entirely of stocks performed best between January 1, 1970 and December 31, 1999, earning 13.7%. But this portfolio was the most volatile, fluctuating with a standard deviation of more than 15%. Surprisingly, an all-bond portfolio was slightly more volatile than one composed of 20% stocks and 80% bonds. In fact, a 40% stock-60% bond portfolio produced 12.2%, or 2.1% more return than the 100% bond portfolio with very little additional volatility. These results are worth studying, while keeping in mind that they may not be repeated in the future.

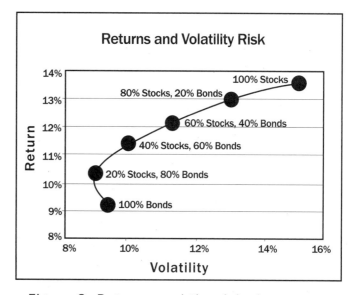

Figure 8: Returns and the risks investors took to get them

Your investment advisor should be able to design a portfolio that matches your risk tolerance and mixes asset classes in proportions that, at least historically, have delivered a yield and volatility suited to your specific goals. If you invest in such a portfolio, keep in mind that past performance is not a predictor of future results. You will have to monitor the portfolio's performance over the years to make sure it continues to produce the returns you require for the success of your retirement plan.

Sample portfolios for different investor goals.

Figure 9 compares an investor's time frame with his or her risk tolerance, to create an appropriate investment mix.

Time frame:	1-5 years	5-10 years	10 or more years
Volatility tolerance **High**	Balanced	Moderate growth	High growth
Volatility tolerance **Medium**	Conservative	Balanced	Moderate growth
Volatility tolerance **Low**	Capital preservation	Conservative	Balanced

Figure 9: Time frame and risk tolerance for different investor goals

Figure 10[42] illustrates the investment mix for each of five portfolios, with information about the returns they produced over the thirty-year period from 1/1/70 to 12/31/99. The *capital preservation* portfolio was a 50%-50% mixture of income-producing bonds and cash equivalents. The *conservative approach* was composed of 30% growth-and-income, 40% income and 30% cash equivalents. The *balanced approach* was composed of 25% each of growth securities, growth-and-income securities, income-producing bonds and cash equivalents. The *moderate approach* was composed of 45% growth securities, 25% growth-and-income securities, 20% income-producing bonds and 10% cash equivalents. The *high growth* portfolio was composed of 70% growth securities, 20% growth-and-income securities and 5% each of income-producing securities and cash equivalents.

Investment:	Capital Preservation	Conservative Approach	Balanced Approach	Moderate Growth	High Growth
Average Annual Return	8.2%	10.2%	11.5%	12.9%	14.0%
Best 5-year return	15.1% (1981-1985)	16.7% (1982-1986)	16.3% (1982-1986)	18.0% (1994-1998)	22.5% (1995-1999)
Worst 5-year return	4.2% (1976-1980)	1.4% (1970-19874)	-2.1% (1970-1974)	-5.9% (1970-1974)	-10% (1970-1974)
Returns were up	28	27	27	24	22
Returns were down	2	3	3	6	8

Figure 10: Sample investment mixes

Figure 10 shows that the more aggressive the portfolio, the higher the average return. If an investor put $2,400 each year into each of the five portfolios and reinvested all distributions, the high growth portfolio would have grown to $984,225, whereas the capital preservation portfolio would have grown to only $ 302,715. This 325% difference in performance by the high growth portfolio was accompanied by greater volatility. As always, you must remember that past performance does not predict future results.

Mutual funds.

Mutual funds have been part of the investment world for nearly eighty years. A mutual fund is an investment company that combines or pools the funds of many individual investors, and issues shares to each investor on a *pro rata* basis. Mutual funds are either "open-end" or "closed-end." An "open-end" fund issues new shares as money comes in. As investors withdraw their money, the fund redeems their shares. "Closed-end" funds are fewer in number, and have a fixed number of shares that are traded on stock exchanges. The Investment Company Act of 1940 closely regulates the mutual fund industry, dictating standards of disclosure, administration, and record keeping.

The proliferation of diverse types of mutual funds has made it easier for investors to construct diversified portfolios.

Growth funds invest in growing companies that tend to keep dividends low and reinvest profits in their own growth. Growth funds can be further subdivided into large or small company funds, foreign, domestic or global funds.

Global or international funds invest in foreign securities, which expose investors to risks not associated with domestic securities. For example, investors in these funds are vulnerable to currency fluctuations, and to political and economic changes.

Growth-and-income funds invest in well-established large companies that have a history of dividends and steady growth. These funds can help to provide steady income in retirement while maintaining the possibility of growth.

Income funds (which include bond funds) and *cash-equivalent funds* (which invest in short-term securities and money markets*) produce interest. Although many people believe that bond funds are completely secure, the value of bonds rises and falls inversely with interest rates. If you sell shares in a bond fund when interest rates have risen, your shares could have decreased in value.

* An investment in a money market fund is not insured nor guaranteed by the Federal Deposit Insurance Corporation or any other government agency. Although such funds seek to preserve the value of the investor's money at $1.00 per share, it is possible to lose money by investing in this type of fund.

Government funds, a type of bond fund, invest in U.S. Government securities. Investors should be aware that the U.S. Government guarantee applies only to the underlying securities in the fund's portfolio, and not to the value of the fund's shares.

High yield bond funds, commonly known as junk bond funds, invest in corporate bonds and are subject to a high level of credit risk and market risk.

Municipal bond funds afford investors certain tax benefits, but these benefits are not assured because of the alternative minimum tax. State and local taxes may also apply to the interest these funds generate. Capital gains distributions from municipal bond funds may also be taxable. Insured municipal bond funds do not offer investors assurance of the value of the fund's shares, but only of the timely payment of principal and interest by the issuer of the underlying securities.

Balanced funds attempt to replicate the entire investment portfolio of the "prudent investor" by investing in stocks and bonds, with the fund managers adjusting the proportion according to market conditions.

Sector funds focus on a particular industry or group of industries, or a geographic area such as the Pacific Rim. Because these sector funds concentrate their investments in narrow segments of the economy, their investors increase their vulnerability to any single economic, political or regulatory development affecting that sector.

With more than 9,000 mutual funds currently on the market, virtually every investor can find a fund that meets his or her specific investment criteria.

People invest in mutual funds for diversification and professional management. If you wish to invest in a specific sector of the global economy, you still have to choose which companies in that sector to invest in. With a limited amount of capital, it is difficult to purchase the shares of more than a handful of companies. However, by purchasing shares in a mutual fund focused on that sector, you acquire shares in numerous companies. The managers of the mutual fund make the investment decisions, and any resulting gains and losses are passed on to the fund's shareholders.

People invest in mutual funds for diversification and professional management.

Some fund families employ a single manager for each fund, while others utilize teams of managers. In the team approach, if one manager leaves, the rest of the team may remain and the strategies continue without interruption. When you examine the historic performance of a fund, make sure that the management team has been in place during that time period. Ten-year performance history is meaningless if the fund's current manager has been there for only two or three years.

What does it cost to purchase and own a mutual fund?

Mutual fund costs break down into two areas: the initial cost to purchase shares and the annual cost to own them. The cost to purchase shares is called the "load," which varies from zero for a no-load fund to several percent of the share value for front-end loaded funds. Front-end loaded funds sell "A" class shares, while back-end loaded funds sell "B" or "C" class shares. B and C class shares have no front-end load but usually have higher annual fees than A shares. Once you decide which fund or funds you wish to purchase, you should then evaluate which share class best meets your objectives.

The load for A shares generally decreases as the amount invested reaches "breakpoints." For example, a fund family that charges a 5.75% load for A shares, for an initial investment of less than

$25,000, may charge only 4.5% at the $100,000 level. The load may vanish at the $1,000,000 level. An investor can indicate at the outset by means of a letter of intent that he or she will make additional investments during the first 13 months that will reach a specified breakpoint. If the total investment meets the "breakpoint" before 13 months have elapsed, the fund charges the lower (breakpoint) load for the entire invest- ment. Back-end loaded funds charge no up-front load but assess higher ongoing fees. If you have purchased shares in one mutual fund, you may generally switch to another fund in the same family without incurring a second load. Rein- vested dividends normally incur no additional load.

The prospectus will list all of the ongoing expenses. The annual management fee may be about 1%. Another fee, called the 12(b)-1 charge, is used to offset marketing and distribution expenses. For A shares, it is generally limited to .75% for domestic funds. For B shares, it could reach 1%. The combination of these annual fees may range up to a few percent.

Many investors do not want to pay an entry fee, and purchase shares in no-load funds. Why pay a load if you do not have to? A load is analogous to points one pays to secure a mort- gage loan. A load is one way to pay a financial planner for helping you develop an investment strategy or a financial plan, and keep it on track. Sometimes, "no load" means "no help." Your planner may suggest the purchase of no-load funds and charge you an annual fee, say 1%, to manage your portfolio.

Sometimes, "no load" means "no help."

Taxation of gains in a mutual fund.

The mutual fund company pays no income taxes on capital gains and dividends. Capital gains and dividends are passed on a *pro rata* basis to the shareholders who incur the tax liability. You (and your accountant) may find it very difficult to calculate your basis or cost for the shares, especially when you reinvest dividends and capital gains.

Investors in mutual funds can incur both ordinary income taxes and capital gains taxes each year. If the shares are held in a non-qualified account, shareholders incur ordinary income taxes on short-term gains that result when a fund manager sells appreciated securities that the fund has held for less than one year. Shareholders should consult qualified tax advisors to determine their tax liability for mutual fund transactions.

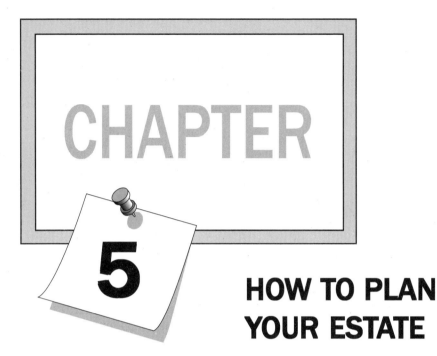

CHAPTER

5

HOW TO PLAN YOUR ESTATE

Each and every person has the opportunity to properly plan for themselves and for their heirs. If you decide to not do any of the planning yourself, you are in effect telling the "system" to do it for you.[43] Unfortunately, the "system" does not always work the way you thought it would, and in the long run family members and heirs suffer the consequences. These consequences frequently involve large estate taxes, and the passage of assets to the wrong people at the wrong time. A word of caution: before proceeding with estate planning,

> Estate planning is not an arena where the amateur can easily succeed.

you must obtain the advice of experienced professionals who are expert in this area of the law. Estate planning is not an arena where the amateur can easily succeed.

Why pay attention to estate planning?

Many people engage in the estate planning process in order to maximize the estate left to survivors and to minimize the tax burden. Keep in mind that taxation is only one of many important facets of estate planning. Estate planning can also address the potential problems of providing estate liquidity. Will there be sufficient liquid assets available to pay estate settlement costs? Can other estate settlement costs be paid from liquid assets? (Liquid assets mean cash, or assets that can quickly be converted to cash.) If there are inadequate liquid assets, will valuable assets have to be sold at a price below their market value just to raise cash? This could result in a forced sale of a business interest, real estate, or securities when the market is depressed.

Estate planning can also insure that there will be sufficient income to maintain the surviving spouse and minor children over a period of many years. Estate planning can also minimize the need to tie up your assets and subject them to the expense and delay caused by probate. It can provide for the care of your minor children and the competent management of their assets.

How estates are taxed.

The following information about estate taxation is general in nature and is not intended as legal or tax advice. The federal government imposes a tax on gifts or bequests of assets from one individual to another. Until 2010, the top tax rates are the same for both types of transfers. Taxes and fees usually must be paid in cash within nine months after a death.

The assets that comprise your taxable estate include your home and other real estate that you own, your bank accounts, your securities (including stocks, bonds and mutual funds), your qualified plan assets (tax- sheltered annuities, pension plan assets and IRAs), and the death benefit proceeds of any life insurance policies that you own. Typically, these assets may grow during a long retirement, and many educators will find that as they near life expectancy, their net worth exceeds the unified credit exemption equivalent. The result could be a heavy estate tax burden on one's heirs. Fortunately, proper planning may reduce or eliminate estate taxes at death.

Aside from estate taxes, other estate settlement costs can reduce the net estate that will eventually pass to your heirs. These costs, which include executor's fees, attorney's charges, accountant's and appraisal fees and probate filing costs, can add substantial expenses to the estate. These are often legitimate and necessary expenses incurred to do "proper planning."

There are two exclusions from estate and gift taxation: the *annual gift tax exclusion* and the *unified credit*.* The law excludes from taxation annual gifts of up to $11,000 in 2003 made by an individual to each of an unlimited number of donees.** This *annual gift tax exclusion*, used year after year to transfer $11,000 to multiple donees, can be a powerful tool for reducing the size of the taxable estate. For example, an individual could gift $11,000 to every family member and friend each year, removing very large sums of money from his or her taxable estate.

* Also called the *credit shelter* amount.

** Donees incur no tax on gifts made to them. Only the donor is subject to taxation, if any.

The *unified credit* exemption equivalent is much larger than the annual exclusion. It is the value of property or assets that every individual can either give away during their lifetime or pass to beneficiaries at their death. Federal estate taxes apply to taxable estates larger than the unified credit exemption equivalent amount.

The unified credit amount is $1,000,000 in 2003. If your estate is at or below this level and you die in 2001, your estate will not incur federal estate tax. A married couple who employs certain planning techniques described below can each shelter the unified credit exemption equivalent amount from taxation, thereby doubling the tax savings.

The unified credit amount is $1,000,000 in 2003.

In the spring of 2001, Congress passed the *Economic Growth and Tax Relief Reconciliation Act of 2001*, which made several important changes in how estates will be taxed in the future. First, the unified credit exemption equivalent is scheduled to increase from $1,000,000 in 2003 to $1,500,000 in 2004-2005, $2,000,000 in 2006-2008 and $3,500,000 in 2009. The 2001 tax act will repeal the estate tax in 2010, but only for one year. In 2011 and later, when the 2001 tax act "sunsets" and ceases to be effective, the unified credit is scheduled to be $1,000,000[44]. The credit against federal estate tax for state estate taxes is also affected by the tax act.[45]

If your estate exceeds the exclusion amount, the tax rate becomes quite steep very quickly, beginning at 37% and increasing to 49%. The estate and gift tax rates are the highest tax rates imposed in the U.S. In the years after 2003, the maximum estate and gift tax rate drops 1% per year until it reaches 45% in 2007. It becomes zero in 2010 and reverts to 55% in 2011 and beyond.

Figure 11 illustrates how the Federal estate and gift tax rates change as the size of the taxable estate increases.

Value of taxable estate	Estate tax
$150,000-$250,000	$38,800+32% of amount over $150,000
$250,000-$500,000	$70,000+34% of amount over $250,000
$500,000-$750,000	$155,800+37% of amount over $500,000
$750,000-$1,000,000	$248,300+39% of amount over $750,000
$1,000,000-$1,250,000	$345,800+41% of amount over $1,000,000
$1,250,000-$1,500,000	$448,300+43% of amount over $1,250,000
$1,500,000-$2,000,000	$555,800+45% of amount over $1,500,000
Above $2,000,000	$780,800+49% of amount over $2,000,000

Figure 11: Federal gift & estate tax for 2003

The probate process.

The process of probate is the judicial administration of only the probate property that passes by will. An individual could become legally incompetent by dying or lose the capacity to function as a result of illness. When you are incompetent in a legal sense, you cannot care for yourself or execute a contract. In that case, the Probate Court will appoint a family member or other qualified individual as conservator or guardian. Underlying the probate process is the assumption that if you really wanted your property to be disposed of in a certain manner, you would have made sure that all the necessary planning documents were properly drafted, executed and updated, prior to your death or disability. In this sense, the court attempts to fulfill the decedent's wishes under the strictest possible interpretation. But this statutory inflexibility can also work to your advantage by ensuring that when you do finally complete a proper estate plan, the plan will be enforced.

When your estate is probated, the court decides the merits of all claims against the estate. It will also determine the rights of all "listed" and "unlisted" beneficiaries. The probate process is designed to give a decedent's creditors a defined period of time to present all claims. The process is open to the public, so that any interested party can read the decedent's will and examine all related documents.

Probate need not be a lengthy, costly or difficult process. It depends on the size and complexity of the estate. Because

Probate need not be a lengthy, costly or difficult process.

there are always fees to be paid, avoiding probate is usually less expensive for the heirs than going through the process.

There are a number of ways to avoid probate. Accounts with named designated beneficiaries (such as IRAs, pension plans, insurance policies, annuities, etc.), automatically avoid probate if you name a plan beneficiary other than your estate. At your death, those beneficiaries may collect the plan assets without the need for a court order or the naming of an executor. Similarly, if you name your intended beneficiary as the joint owner of your account, then upon your death that individual will automatically take over your entire account.

Popular estate planning strategies.

A proper estate plan should consider a variety of issues, many of which are reflected in these documents:

- Last Will and Testament

- Pour-over will

- QTIP Trust

- Living Trust

- Durable Powers of Attorney

- Living Will and Healthcare Proxy

- Unified Credit Shelter Trust

- Irrevocable Life Insurance Trust

- Charitable bequests

When properly utilized, each estate planing strategy may provide you with specific and important benefits. You might begin planning your estate by selecting an attorney who will listen closely to your dispositive wishes, help you choose from among the available strategies, and draft and execute the relevant documents. Before acting on your attorney's suggestions, you may wish to involve other advisors, such as your accountant and a life insurance professional experienced in estate planning, in discussions with your attorney. You should fully explain your situation to all of your advisors and these advisors must be willing and able to work with each other.

Every advisor should strive to gain a macro-view of your situation, so that each can make an informed and coordinated decision in your best interest.

The simple will

A basic or simple will leaves everything to a surviving spouse, children or other heirs. This is why it is sometimes called an "I love you " will. If you use this type of will to leave your estate to your spouse and you have a sufficiently large estate and made no taxable gifts during life, you will forfeit the use of the unified credit. By employing a simple will, only the second spouse to die will be able to employ his or her credit.*

* See the description below of the credit shelter trust, which enables both spouses to use their unified credits.

By executing a simple will, your survivors will avoid the consequences of the intestacy process. Each state's intestacy statute provides a state-created will for those individuals who die without a valid will that reflects their specific wishes.** The intestacy laws typically provide for a spouse and children in specified proportions.

> By executing a simple will, your survivors will avoid the consequences of the intestacy process.

**The intestacy statute does not apply to property passing by contract or deed.

You probably would not consider giving your child or grandchild $1,000,000 outright while you are alive and able to provide some guidance and control in spending the money. The legal system assumes that if you did not want to give the bequest outright to minors, you would have done something about it. Therefore, it is prudent to execute a valid will and update it as circumstances change. If you die without such a will, the intestacy laws will give your beneficiary his or her total inheritance at age 18.

You must decide who is best able to raise your children if should you die while they are minors. You should consider the suitability of potential guardians from several aspects: the ages of proposed guardians and their children; the ages of your minor children and the health and financial situation of all parties. Since your first choice of guardian may decline to serve, plan to develop a list of suitable alternates. Remember that circumstances change. If you name a married couple as guardians and one of them dies, would you want the surviving co-guardian to act as the sole guardian? What if the guardians divorce? Consider which co-guardian you prefer, or whether you would want the divorced co-guardians to serve.

Assume that all or part of your estate passes through probate. You need to choose an executor. The executor plays an important and often time-consuming role in the probate process. Select this individual or corporate entity carefully. Among the executor's many duties, he or she assembles and manages the

You need to choose an executor.

decedent's assets, has them appraised, sells any personal property of the decedent and distributes them as specified in the will. These duties can require much work, and may overwhelm a spouse serving as executor who has just lost his or her mate. Since this job is so difficult and demanding, you may choose to appoint a trust company to handle these responsibilities.

If you have a trust, either in your will, a separate lifetime irrevocable trust or living trust, you will need to name a trustee to manage investments, pay taxes, make distributions, etc. In the event he or she dies, you will want to provide for one or more successor trustees.

Executors and trustees are referred to as fiduciaries because of the higher standard of care that is required of them in managing the assets of another person. Unlike people, corporate executors and trustees do not die or become disabled. They are financially accountable for their errors. Unlike friends or relatives who tend to make distributions every time the children ask for something, corporate fiduciaries are impartial and detached. They are supposed to keep current with the constant changes in the law and have investment, accounting and tax expertise.

Should you choose an individual or corporate fiduciary? An individual fiduciary may be a relative or friend who may not charge a fee, and may have a personal interest in the well being of the minors. Frequently, an individual is chosen because of his or her special expertise (i.e., running the family business). You may wish to appoint both an individual and a corporate trustee as co-trustees, to obtain the advantages of each.

You need to decide how you want assets distributed to your children. Your assets should be held in a trust if you do not want them distributed outright to your children at age 18 or 21 in the event of your demise. The trustee will take care of their needs as instructed by the trust provisions. However, at some future time you will probably want the trust to distribute the assets to your children. You can arrange for the trust to distribute the estate gradually over time. For example, you may direct the trust to begin distributions when your child reaches age 21 and continue these distributions until, say, the child reaches age 30. You can design any distribution schedule you desire. You may direct the trust to make lump sum distributions when and if certain benchmarks are reached, for example, when the beneficiary earns a graduate degree.

You should decide in advance to whom you want your estate to pass in the event that your children pass away prior to inheriting your estate. For example, you may want to divide the estate between the husband's and wife's sides of the family, or you may wish to specify a charitable bequest (see below).

Revocable and irrevocable trusts.

A trust is a legal relationship in which one party — the trustee — holds and administers property for the benefit of another — the beneficiary. You can create an intervivos trust during your lifetime to hold your assets (either an irrevocable or a revocable (living) trust), or you can direct your will to create a trust at your death (a "testamentary" trust).

You direct the placement of assets into a living trust.

You direct the placement of assets into a living trust. Living trusts permit you, the grantor, to change the terms of the trust at will. You can add or remove property from the living trust, change the beneficiaries and how assets will be distributed to them. The living trust offers no direct estate tax savings.* To remove property from your estate (and possible taxation at your death), you must relinquish all control of the gifted property. The IRS does not consider property that you place into a revocable living

* It is possible to realize tax savings from a living trust, by keeping the details of an estate secret. If the estate goes through the probate process, which is public, potential purchasers of estate property may gain financial information that would place them in a superior bargaining position with the heirs.

trust as a completed gift for estate tax and gift tax purposes because you have the power to amend the trust during your lifetime. Your gifts of property into the trust are "incomplete," and any assets remaining in your living trust will be subject to estate taxes after your death.

The living trust creates a procedure whereby your chosen representatives will have control of your assets so that they can handle them as you have dictated in the event of your death, disability, or incompetence. Thus, the living trust is an estate-planning document that operates both while you are alive and after you have died.

Many people consider probate avoidance to be the major advantage of the living trust. By avoiding the probate process, your representatives can eliminate delays, retain family privacy and potentially save administration costs. The living trust will also avoid the interruption of income for family members upon the death, disability or incompetence of the person establishing it.*

* The properly drafted living trust may also serve to protect assets in the event of a placement in a nursing home. The trust can provide a safe receptacle for estate assets, for death benefits from qualified pension and employee benefit plans, and perhaps even for insurance proceeds in the case of a smaller estate.

The living trust is often called a "will substitute." Upon the creator's death the trust can divide into various shares to qualify for the state and federal marital deduction, take advantage of the federal unified tax credit, make charitable bequests, or just distribute the assets outright, depending on the creator's wishes.

By contrast, if you place assets into a properly designed irrevocable trust and live three additional years, you may avoid estate taxation on those assets upon your death. Your will may also direct that at your death, part or all of your estate should be held by a trustee in trust for various family members or other beneficiaries. Since this trust does not come into existence until your death, it is called a "testamentary trust." A testamentary trust describes how these assets will be distributed to beneficiaries. A lifetime gift into an irrevocable trust, however, requires you to file a federal gift tax return, depending on the amount that is gifted into the trust, the terms and conditions of the trust and the rights of the beneficiaries. You do, however, generally surrender your legal right to control the property that has been placed into an irrevocable trust.

The Pour-over Will.

The pour-over will is a simple will that provides for your living trust to be your sole beneficiary for any assets that were not placed in your living trust by the time of your death. In other words, if any assets were not placed in your living trust during your lifetime, your will directs that they be "poured over" into your living trust.

You will need a pour-over will even if you transferred all of your assets to a living trust. The pour-over will assures that if your estate receives assets after your death these assets will end up in the living trust.

The QTIP Trust.

QTIP is an acronym for "qualified terminable interest property." This type of trust allows the first spouse to die to specify who will receive his or her assets after the surviving spouse dies. Use of a QTIP trust also permits the deferral of estate taxes on the assets until the death of the surviving spouse.

The Qualified Domestic Trust.

Transfers at death to a non-citizen spouse will not qualify for the marital deduction unless the assets pass to a qualified domestic trust (QDOT). The QDOT rules require a U .S. trustee (unless waived by the IRS). This helps to ensure that the IRS will collect estate taxes owed when principal is removed from the QDOT, or at the surviving non-citizen spouse's later demise.

The Living Will.

Most states permit an adult whose death is imminent to decide whether or not he or she wants healthcare providers to use life-sustaining procedures. The living will documents that determination in writing. Right-to-die statutes establish laws that acknowledge the rights of mature individuals to decide on the nature of their medical care. They may choose to decline life-sustaining procedures that might cause them unwanted pain and suffering. You can revoke your living will whenever you wish by destroying or directing the destruction of the document or by signing a written revocation.

The Durable Power Of Attorney.

A durable power of attorney appoints another individual to handle your affairs for you.* It enables someone to act in your place when you are physically unable to act for yourself, (for example, if you are in a

* Significant powers may be granted under a power of attorney. Before using a pre-printed form, as with all strategies described here, you should obtain competent legal advice before executing the document.

coma) either with respect to your assets or healthcare decisions. For instance, when a person is in a coma, and is not able to deal with any of his or her affairs, the power of attorney can be a simple straightforward way of enabling someone else to handle matters. One can also utilize a power of attorney to have someone sign a stock certificate, take care of a house closing, etc., when the person who executed the power is unable to be present when documents are to be signed.

Your power of attorney should specifically describe how and in what circumstances you want matters handled, with all the details. If you are deemed incapable, a court may appoint a close family member to handle your affairs whom you would not normally choose. By executing a valid durable power of attorney, you can avoid this potential situation.

The Springing Durable Power Of Attorney for Healthcare Decisions

The springing durable power of attorney appoints a family member or friend to make healthcare decisions according to your wishes when you are unable do so. You may either allow medical service providers to have unlimited freedom to act, or you may choose to appoint another person through the springing

durable power of attorney with whom the medical staff must consult. The "springing durable
power of attorney" is designed to become opera-
tional only if and when you become incapaci-
tated, and eliminates the worry that the holder
of the power will act without your knowledge or
wishes while you are still competent.

The Credit Shelter Trust.

Current tax law permits a decedent to pass
an unlimited amount of money or property (the
unlimited marital deduction) to a surviving spouse
without taxation if the surviving spouse is a U.S.
citizen. Suppose a married couple has executed a
simple will. Under the terms of such a will the
surviving spouse will receive the decedent's
assets under the *unlimited marital deduction*. The
first spouse to die has, in effect, wasted his or
her unified credit, assuming that he or she made
no taxable gifts while alive. In this case, only the
survivor may utilize his or her unified credit at
death. If both spouses wish to use their credits,
thereby sheltering (in 2003) $2,000,000 from
federal estate taxation, they should employ a
credit shelter trust. This trust may be created
while the spouses are alive, or through the will
at the first death (a testamentary credit shelter
trust). They could also leave their assets outright
to their children at the first death.

The *testamentary* credit shelter trust can provide lifetime benefits to the surviving spouse, without having those trust assets included in the survivor's estate at his or her subsequent death. The surviving spouse can receive annual income from the trust, and have certain limited rights to invade the trust principal without exposing the trust assets to estate taxation. The *living* credit shelter trust avoids probate and also helps to ensure that both spouses use their unified credit. A married couple using this type of trust can, if they have sufficient assets, pass twice the unified credit amount to children or other heirs, without probate expense or estate tax.

The Irrevocable Life Insurance Trust for a Married Couple.

Every life insurance policy has an owner, an insured individual and a beneficiary or beneficiaries. Although life insurance proceeds paid to the beneficiary at the insured's death are generally not subject to state and federal income taxes, the proceeds are included for estate tax purposes in the policyholder's estate. One may avoid estate taxation of life insurance death benefits by arranging for a trust to own the policy and to be the beneficiary of the death proceeds. This type of trust, called *an irrevocable life insurance trust,* cannot be altered after its creation. The grantor cannot remove assets from the trust.

Funded Irrevocable Insurance Trusts

The grantor of a funded irrevocable life insurance trust transfers income-producing assets into it so that the income will pay the premiums on an insurance policy. Irrevocable life insurance trusts are typically not funded because the gift taxes on the assets transferred are the same as the federal estate taxes on assets remaining in the estate. Also, the income earned on the assets would in most cases still be included on the income tax return of the insured grantor.

Unfunded Irrevocable Insurance Trusts

This trust usually owns just an insurance policy and the grantor makes annual gifts to the trust with which the trustee can pay the premiums.[46]

Charitable bequests.

You may reduce a future estate tax bill by making a charitable bequest. Charitable giving techniques such as the *charitable remainder trust*, under the right circumstances, may create income tax savings and increased cash flow for the donor. They accomplish this by converting a non-income-producing asset that has appreciated, and which if sold would trigger a tax, to a tax write-off and a lifetime income stream. For example, you may own stock that has greatly appreciated but pays no dividends. You may have a need or desire for additional income at some point. You may be reluctant to sell appreciated shares because of the taxes that event would generate, which would reduce the gain you would realize.

If you create a charitable remainder trust and donate the stock to this trust, you will receive a current tax deduction. If the charity then sells the appreciated stock, no income or capital gain tax is triggered. The charity can then invest the entire proceeds of the sale to produce a lifetime income stream for you and your family. This income is subject to income taxes. It could be larger than had you sold the stock, paid the tax and invested the remaining proceeds in income-producing assets. You may be concerned about replacing the value of the gifted asset for your heirs. You may use a portion of the tax deduction and/or some of the additional income to pay premiums on a life insurance policy that would replace the monetary value of the donated asset for your heirs. Besides the financial advantages of charitable giving, donors usually

enjoy the positive feelings that come from helping others and the expression of appreciation
from the charitable entity and the community at
large.

Second-To-Die Life Insurance Policies.

Favorite tools of estate planners, second-to-
die life insurance policies, are designed to provide estate liquidity at the second death. The
trustee of an irrevocable life insurance trust
usually purchases a second-to-die insurance
death benefit based on a calculation of the potential estate tax to be replaced. Because the trust
owns the policy, the death proceeds are not
includable in the deceased couple's estates.

Because two people must die before the
death benefit is triggered, these policies generally have lower premiums than single-life policies for the same death benefit. The lower premium accounts in part for the popularity of
second-to-die policies.

In recent years, some planners have ques-
tioned whether these policies are necessarily the
bargain they appear to be. As with any life
insurance policy, the second-to-die policy is
most cost-effective if both insureds die prematurely. Insurance companies are now marketing

new forms of this policy, such as variable universal second-to-die. Before purchasing such a policy, make sure you examine the underlying assumptions concerning mortality and longevity. When the first spouse dies, the surviving spouse is still required to pay premiums. If the surviving spouse lives to a ripe old age, he or she may find it burdensome to pay premiums. Ask your planner to help you determine whether purchasing a single life policy on the younger spouse, older spouse, or both equally would be the best deal.

AFTERWORD

Beyond the financial strategies I have described in this book, I want to share two non-financial ideas about our beliefs and our capacity for gratitude that I have found useful in both my professional and personal life. I hope they will help you as well.

Changing your beliefs can help you.

We have accumulated our beliefs over a lifetime of experience. Many of our beliefs date back to our childhood, when we listened to our parents talking over the dinner table. We acquired other beliefs in the schoolyard from our friends. Some beliefs that we adopted as children may be less useful in our adult lives. Did you know that you could change your beliefs and adopt new ones that better suit your present needs?

Beliefs take two forms: *rules beliefs* and *global beliefs*. A rules belief tells you the "correct" action to take in a particular circumstance: *"If you are my friend and I am sick, then you will call me every day."* Global beliefs express universal truths: *"All people are created equal."*

Each of us has a unique set of rules and global beliefs about money. Some are useful and

some get in the way. In my seminars, I frequently meet people who tell me: "I will never
be able to retire in comfort," or "no matter how
hard I work, I can't save money." Sometimes
they express a global belief: "People like us
never get rich." We pay a price for carrying
around negative beliefs. If you have negative
beliefs about money, you may benefit by getting
in touch with the stress that these beliefs create
in your daily life. They may diminish your self-
confidence, your enthusiasm or your ability to
take on new challenges.

Would you like to change your negative
beliefs? Try this little exercise. Imagine yourself
five years older and you are still carrying these
negative beliefs on your back like a heavy sack of
potatoes. Look into an imaginary mirror five
years in the future. Do you look older or
younger? What is missing in your life as a result
of carrying those negative beliefs? Was your
energy enhanced or diminished by those beliefs?
Now imagine walking another five years into the
future. You are ten years older. Again, look into
the mirror. Do you like what you see? What
pleasures and experiences have you missed
because you held tightly to this negative belief?
(If this exercise makes you uncomfortable, it is
working.) Now, come back to the present. Write
down the opposites of your negative beliefs.
Study them for a few moments. Take another

trip into the future, this time without the weight of the negative beliefs. Look into the mirror and see how your life has changed for the better because you got rid of the negative beliefs. You can do this exercise with each limiting or negative belief you discover, and in so doing you can develop a new belief system about money that better serves your purposes.

Practice being grateful every day

I hope that this book helps you to create, protect and enjoy your money. However, financial success does not necessarily correlate with happiness. Have you ever read or heard about a financially successful person who was unhappy? We are aware of many examples of successful people who could not deal with their success. Some even ended their lives. I believe that we balance our increasing financial success with an increased conscious expression of gratitude.

When we become grateful for someone or something, at that moment we *appreciate* it. In financial terms, if an asset appreciates, its value increases. By appreciating someone or something, you increase its value and meaning, not just to yourself but also to everyone around you. Why is it important to practice the habit of gratitude? We never succeed in a vacuum. *Our capacity to succeed correlates with our ability to be grateful to the people and circumstances that helped us achieve that success.*

If we look closely at our lives each day, we may discover that we have so much to be grateful for. Gratitude can either be reactive or conscious. We may react by being grateful when someone comes to our aid in an emergency, or helps us without our having asked. We are always capable of reactive gratitude. In contrast, we must adopt and practice the habit of conscious gratitude. Very few people choose each day to appreciate their life, values, teachers, talents, and opportunities. We may benefit by consciously appreciating the multitude of people and circumstances that make our lives richer and more valuable. These may include the ongoing flow of small, pleasurable and meaningful everyday events, such as a student's expression of gratitude for our help. Or it may be the realization that we spend our professional lives in a magnificent career that enriches everyone with whom we interact. I believe that the more consciously grateful we are, the more success we will have in life. If we develop the daily habit of appreciating how fortunate we are to live in our free society, with its infinite value, variety and opportunity, we may open ourselves to greater success.

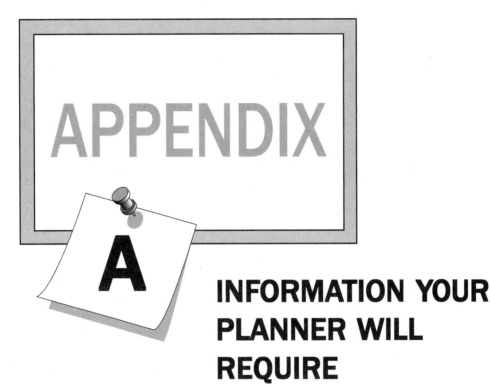

APPENDIX

A

INFORMATION YOUR PLANNER WILL REQUIRE

You should be prepared to provide photocopies of these documents to your planner:

- Teachers' Retirement System current statement.

- Most recent payroll stubs.

- A detailed monthly budget based on two or three years' experience.

- Income tax returns for the past three years.

- Personal employment benefit statements.

- School district benefit plan booklets.

- Names and addresses of your attorney, investment counselor, accountant, and all insurance agents.

- Your will and trust arrangements, including names of trustees and guardians.

- Business ownership arrangements.

- Insurance contracts, including life, health, long-term care, property and casualty, liability, disability, and major medical policies.

- Annuity contracts and statements.

- Investment and savings account statements.

- Retirement plan account statements.

- Property ownership arrangements. You should be prepared to discuss these issues with the planner, and any others relevant to your specific situation.

- Present liabilities, including pending lawsuits.

- Anticipated inheritances.

- Anticipated education expenses both for children and parents.

- Anticipated financial obligations, such as supporting a family member.

- Anticipated change in employment status.

- What you would most love to do in retirement.

- Possessions you wish to acquire, such as a vacation home.

- Any other financial information, whether fact or feelings that you consider relevant.

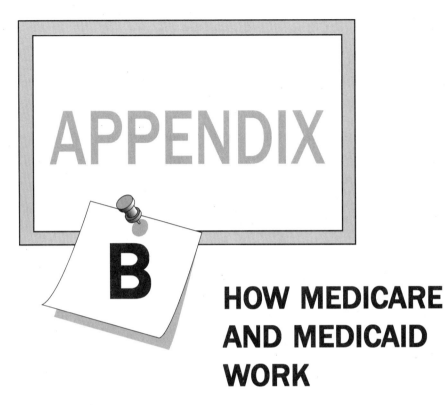

APPENDIX

B

HOW MEDICARE AND MEDICAID WORK

Medicare

Medicare Part A is hospital insurance and covers costs associated with confinement in a skilled nursing facility or a hospital.[47]

Part A will cover skilled services in a nursing home for up to 100 days, if you meet these requirements:

1. You have been hospitalized for at least three consecutive days;

2. In most cases, you enter a Medicare approved skilled nursing facility within 30 days after discharge, and

3. You are receiving skilled care (which includes services such as physical therapy, injections, catheterization, etc).

If you meet *and continue to meet* these three requirements, Medicare will cover all eligible expenses for skilled care for the first twenty days, all but $105 a day for the next 80 days. The individual pays all costs beyond the 100th day in the benefit period.[48] However, some patients receiving care in nursing homes are not receiving skilled care, and some who initially need skilled care quickly "downgrade" to intermediate or custodial care, thereby losing their Medicare benefit.

Medicare Part A also covers part-time or intermittent skilled care in the home, including home health aide services, durable medical supplies and other services. This care is supposed to be unlimited, but in practice is limited to occasional visits. If the patient is considered likely to recover, Medicare pays for some custodial care. Medicare will cover up to 100 days per benefit period for skilled nursing home care confinement.

Medicaid.

Medicaid pays for nursing home care for those who are impoverished. States have strict Medicaid eligibility rules requiring individuals to spend down assets to the poverty level in order to qualify for aid. *In other words, you may keep only minimal assets in order to receive Medicaid long-term care coverage.*

Many states have a cap on how much wealth you can retain. For example, a single person in NY can keep a few thousand dollars (the amount varies by state and in 2001 is $3,850 in New York), a prepaid funeral of any amount, a car, and term life insurance. If the individual's earnings are less than the cost of nursing care, Medicaid allows this person to keep only a few dollars for personal expenses in an account in the nursing home (this amount is $50 in New York).

How are assets treated? The assets of both spouses are combined for purposes of Medicaid eligibility, even if you are in a second or third marriage. Consider the implications of this rule. Say that an older man marries for the second time, perhaps because he is looking for someone to care for him later in life. If he chooses a younger wife who has assets of her own, Medicaid treats her assets as if they were his, even if they had a prenuptial agreement that kept their assets separate.

Medicaid also sets a limit on how much the community spouse (the one remaining at home) can earn without disqualifying the Medicaid recipient. In New York, for the ill spouse to qualify for a Medicaid-paid nursing home bed, the couple must pay for care until their assets and income reach certain thresholds. The community spouse may retain the home, an income of up to $2,266.50 per month, the family car, and personal belongings. The community spouse may petition Medicaid for more income if necessary to maintain the household.

Medicaid "look back" rules.

Often one hears this story: My *grandmother entered a nursing home in the late 1970's after having transferred her wealth, and Medicaid paid for over five years of care. Can my parents do the same?*

Times have changed. Over the past decade, Medicaid, a joint Federal/State program, has imposed increasingly strict eligibility rules. Today, when you apply for nursing home care under Medicaid the "look back" period extends for 36 months. If you made any gifts (or transfers for less than full market value) you could be ineligible for Medicaid benefits for up to 36 months, depending on how much you gifted. (If you applied for Medicaid within the waiting period and were deemed ineligible, your waiting period could, in some situations, be extended beyond the 36-month cap.)

Can you make your assets inaccessible to Medicaid?

Any transfer of assets creates a period of ineligibility. During this period, which can last as long as three years, you are disqualified for Medicaid assistance. Medicaid will take a hard look at your last three years of financial records. To determine the length of this ineligibility period in months, divide the amount you gifted by the average monthly cost of nursing care in your area as determined by your state department of welfare. For example, if you gave away $90,000 and nursing home care costs $6,000 a month where you live, the disqualification period is $90,000 divided by $6,000 or 15 months. If you gave half of this money to your children, you would be ineligible for benefits for 7.5 months.

When you give away assets to qualify for Medicaid, you incur a host of other problems. You may have to pay both state and federal gift taxes, and may utilize part of your unified credit.

The recipients of your gifts will retain your old basis, so that when they sell the appreciated assets, they will incur income taxes. You lose control over gifted assets, no matter how careful you are to structure your gifts. If your lawyer* has advised you to give away assets to your children, did the lawyer also ask if your children had good, sound marriages? If you gift to married children who later divorce, a child may lose half of the asset to the departing spouse. In the case of a lawsuit, a child could lose the whole asset.

As the number of older Americans has increased, some attorneys have focused their practice on the special planning needs and pressing issues that their older clients must contend with. This relatively new Elder Law practice includes areas such as managing long term care, Medicaid, Medicare, Social Security, planning for disability, tax and estate planning, living wills, guardianships, conservatorships, and combating discrimination against the elderly.

What about Medicaid-avoidance trusts?

Section 1917(d) of the Social Security Act states "where an individual, his or her spouse, or anyone acting on the individual's behalf, establishes a trust using at least some of the individual's funds, that trust can be considered available to the individual for purpose of determining eligibility for Medicaid."[49] If your attorney tells you that a certain type of trust arrangement will work, ask for a written guarantee. Medicaid has a 5-year look back for some trusts. If your Medicaid-qualifying trust was written before 1993, there are new rules that do not grandfather these old trusts. Any irrevocable trust with provisions to return income to the grantor, or where the grantor is a beneficiary, cannot shield assets from Medicaid. Any asset that is retained in your taxable estate is deemed subject to state liens to recover Medicaid costs.

Is your home safe from Medicaid?

If you are single and spend more than nine months in a nursing home under Medicaid, and cannot return home for medical reasons, you must sell your house. There are exceptions to this rule.* If you are married, the at-home spouse may continue to live in your house.

* There will be no Medicaid lien on the house if it is occupied by the spouse, a minor child, a disabled or blind child of any age, or a sibling with an equity interest who lived in the home for at least one year. You may also transfer the house immediately to an adult child who spent two years supporting and caring for the disabled parent.

If you are a Medicaid patient in a nursing home and return to the hospital for more than 30 days, you may forfeit your bed. Then you are obliged to take the next vacant Medicaid bed, which may turn out to be located far from your loved ones. The bottom line: Medicaid is not the best answer to long-term care protection.

AN OVERVIEW OF SOCIAL SECURITY BENEFITS

Eligibility.

In most cases, you need 10 years or 40 quarters of work to qualify for the Social Security retirement benefit. The earliest you can collect the retirement benefit is age 62. However, the benefit at 62 is a reduced benefit, determined by the age at which you would be eligible for a full Social Security benefit. That age is related to your year of birth as shown in Figure 12.

Year of birth	Normal retirement age
Before 1938	65
1938	65 & 2 months
1939	65 & 4 months
1940	65 & 6 months
1941	65 & 8 months
1942	65 & 10 months
1943-1954	66
1955	66 & 2 months
1956	66 & 4 months
1957	66 & 6 months
1958	66 & 8 months
1959	66 & 10 months
1960 & after	67

Figure 12: Normal retirement age for Social Security benefits

Benefit calculation

The amount of your monthly Social Security benefit is based on your earnings covered by Social Security throughout your working history. Your earnings up to the maximum tax by Social

Security are considered and earlier salaries are adjusted to reflect changes in average wage levels over the year you have worked. The maximum number of years used in the calculation is 35. The earnings are averaged together and a formula is applied to determine the primary insurance amount.

Early retirement.

If you are eligible for full benefits at age 65, you will receive 80% of the full benefit if you collect at age 62. The full retirement age will increase from 65 and 2 months for people born in 1938, to age 67 for people born in 1960 and later. As the age of full benefit increases, the reduction of benefits at age 62 will also increase. Individuals born in the period from 1943 to 1954 will receive 75% of full benefits at age 62. A retiree eligible for full benefits at age 67 will receive 70% of that benefit at age 62.

Your Average Indexed Monthly Earnings (AIME) determines the size of your monthly benefit. For example, if you were born in 1940 and you qualified for 100% Primary Insurance Amount (PIA), and your AIME were at the maximum level, your age-65 and 6 months benefit would be $1,729 in 2005. If you elected the age-62 benefit, the monthly payment would drop to $1,305. Taking benefits at age 62 results in a difference of $404 per month. However, because you would receive the reduced payments 3.5 years earlier, you will be ahead of the game for several years, enjoying an earlier stream of monthly benefits. You can calculate your potential monthly benefit at early or full retirement ages by accessing Social Security's website,[50] which also provides detailed information about the other aspects of Social Security.

Reviewing your Earnings and Benefit Estimate Statement.

You should begin the review of your Social Security benefits by obtaining your personal earnings and benefit estimates statement. [51] When your statement arrives, you should first check the listing of your earnings that were subject to Social Security taxes and the amount of tax you actually paid. If errors have been made and there are zeros in years when you had earnings and paid into Social Security, you should contact Social Security. Corrections will be made if you can provide W-2 statements, pay stubs or other proof. It is a good idea to check with Social Security every three years to make sure that your records are accurate. Your estimate will show your benefits at age 62, your full retirement age, and age 70.

As a rule, early retirement will give you your full benefits over your lifetime, but the checks will be smaller since you will receive them over a longer period. If you cannot work because of poor health, you may be eligible for disability benefits, which are the same amount as full, unreduced retirement benefits.

Spousal and family benefits.

A spouse receives benefits based either on his or her employment record, or half of the other spouse's benefits, whichever is greater. This assumes that the working spouse waited until age 65 to begin collecting benefits. A spouse collecting benefits at age 62 would receive 37.5% of the worker's age 65 benefits. A married couple, both of whom had made the maximum contributions to Social Security, will each receive the maximum benefit. An unmarried divorced spouse may also receive benefits if the couple was married for at least ten years.

Other benefits.

If you become disabled, and the disability has lasted or is expected to last for least twelve months, and if you have five years of coverage in the last ten years prior to the disability, you and your dependents can receive Social Security benefits. Survivor benefits are also paid to certain members of the worker's family, and a lump sum payment of $255 is paid to a surviving spouse or entitled child.

Social Security taxes.

Both you and your employer pay the Social Security tax rate of 7.65% of the first $80,400 of your earnings, plus an extra Medicare tax of 1.45% of all earnings above $87,000. In the future, the tax rate is expected to remain the same, but the wage base will rise.

Taxation of Social Security benefits.

If you are receiving a pension from employment where you paid Social Security taxes, the pension will not affect your Social Security benefits. After you reach age 65, you can have unlimited earnings and still collect full Social Security benefits.[52] Retirees with other income may have to pay taxes on their Social Security benefit, as follows:

If you file an individual federal tax return, and your base amount (modified adjusted gross income plus ½ of your Social Security benefits received in the taxable year) is $25,000 to $34,000, you may have to pay taxes on up to 50% of your Social Security benefits. If your base amount is above $34,000, up to 85% of your Social Security benefits is subject to income tax.

If you file a joint return, you may have to pay taxes on up to 50% of your benefits if you and your spouse have a combined base amount between $32,000 and $44,000. If your combined base amount is more than $44,000, up to 85% of your Social Security benefits are subject to income taxation.

If you are married filing separately and have not lived apart from your spouse for the entire taxable year, your base amount is zero, and 85% of your Social Security benefits will be taxable.[53]

The safety net of Social Security may not be there for us in the future. Even if we are counting on Social Security as part of our retirement income, we have to take responsibility for our financial futures.

FOOTNOTES

[1] U.S. Bureau of the Census, Survey of Income and Program Participation.

[2] See "A Lawyer's Workbook," *The New York Times*, November 11, 2001 Section 2, p.1 for a detailed discussion of the process many attorneys are currently using to determine the monetary awards they are seeking for victims of the Sept. 11th tragedy. They attempt to quantify in monetary terms the "pain and suffering" the event caused family members.

[3] Employee Benefit Research Institute, Issue Brief No.163, July 1995.

[4] Janet Gemignani, "The Dollars and Sense of Covering Long-term Care," *Business and Health*, February 1996, p.55.

[5] Employee Benefit Research Institute, Issue Brief No. 163, July 1995.

[6] U.S. Department of Commerce, Census Brief, CENBR 97-5, issued December 1997.

[7] Room and board cost only based on 2001 CNA "Cost of Nursing Care study."

[8] MetLife study, "2000 Nursing Home Cost Survey."

[9] A study by Samuel X. Kaplan, "The Case for Self-Funding, Corporate-Sponsored, Employee-Paid Long term Care Benefits," *Compensation and Benefits Review*, May/June 1995, p.52, revealed that after paying for one year of long-term care, 72% of elderly Americans were impoverished. Another study entitled "Serious Ills Hit Family Savings" (*Business & Health*, February 1995, p.13) found that 31% of families reported that they had depleted a large part of all of their savings to pay for long-term care.

[10] *Statistical Abstracts of the United States*, 2000 edition, p. 84.

[11] Healthcare Financing Administration, National Health Expenditures, Table 9, **www.hcfa.gov/stats/nhe-oact/tables/t17.htm**.

[12] General Accounting Office, Testimony Before the Special Committee on Aging, U.S. Senate, March 9, 1998.

[13] Some insurers accelerate this benefit by permitting the insured to use a week's worth of home care benefits in one day.

[14] Alzheimer's Disease or senile dementia.

[15] Eating, dressing, continence, transferring from bed to chair, toileting and bathing.

[16] Human assistance with the ADLs may include active personal assistance, supervisory assistance or directional assistance.

[17] One provider permits virtually any modification of the patient's home that will allow the patient to stay in the home (thus, avoiding costly nursing home care). This provider will build an elevator for the patient, or install a "smart floor" which monitors and reports the blood pressure and heartbeat of an individual who has fallen and cannot get up off the floor.

[18] See Figure 1, p. 37 for details.

[19] You may obtain a copy of *A Shopper's Guide to Long-Term Care Insurance,* which contains these worksheets, by writing to the National Association of Insurance Commissioners, 120 West 12th Street, Site 1100, Kansas City, MO 64105-1925. You may call them at 816-842-3600 or e-mail them at ***www.naic.org.***

[20] Some states such as Pennsylvania also offer a money purchase method, which applies a factor to the member's account balance to determine the pension benefit. The retirement system makes annual deposits that accrue in the member's account. At retirement, the system applies a factor to the member's account balance to compute the pension benefit. Pennsylvania computes the retirement benefit by both the formula and money purchase methods. The retiree receives the larger benefit.

[21] This is not the case in every state, and you need to learn your state retirement system's rules regarding changing beneficiaries during retirement.

[22] This calculation is based on current New York State Teachers Retirement System option factors for a Tier 1 or Tier 2 retiree.

[23] This value was calculated in July of 2003 using then current factors, including mortality rates and interest rates. These factors change with time. Therefore, when using the annuity method for calculating how much life insurance death benefit is necessary to replicate a joint-and-survivor pension, one should use current rates.

[24] Data from Ibbetson Associates, *Stocks, Bonds, Bills and Inflation Yearbook*- Cash equivalents: U.S. Treasury Bill Index 1970-1996 from CRSP Government Bond File and 1977-1999 from *The Wall Street Journal*; Bonds: Salomon Smith Barney Long-Term High-Grade Corporate Bond Index; Stocks: the S&P 500; Inflation: Consumer Price Index.

[25] All examples are hypothetical and cannot be used to predict the results of any particular product or strategy.

[26] This sum is calculated as follows: This option pays Molly $31,565 per year after John dies. If we divide $31,565 by 4% we get $798,125 as the required lump sum to be invested. Keep in mind that unless the interest rate is guaranteed, the retiree and survivor may not be able to achieve this rate throughout their retirement.

[27] You can obtain an estimate of your projected option losses for a particular retirement date from your state teachers' retirement system. The website www.state.ne.us/home/pers/publicret.htm contains links to every state retirement system, and many states provide retirement calculators (including option calculators) on their sites.

[28] As described earlier, whole life policies provide minimum guaranteed cash values, which are independent of annual dividends. Check policy illustrations for tables of guaranteed and projected (non-guaranteed) cash values.

[29] Term insurance premiums generally increase as the insured individual ages. Term insurance policies do not build cash values. The policy simply provides a death benefit for a given period of time. Premiums may be level for a set period (5, 10 and 15 year periods are common) or may increase each year (yearly renewable term). At older ages term premiums become very costly.

[30] A.M. Best Company: (900) 420-0400. Fitch, Inc.: (312) 368-3157. Moody's Investor Service, Inc.: (212) 553-1653. Standard & Poor's: (212) 208-1527. Weiss Research, Inc.: (800) 289-9222.

[31] Loan interest is partially offset by interest accrued on the borrowed funds. The net cost of the loan in most contracts is about 1%. Outstanding loans will decrease the death benefit dollar for dollar.

[32] For 2001, we calculate this by multiplying the years of service (not to exceed 10) by 20% of taxable income, then subtracting previous contributions. The result is the special "year of separation" deferral limit.

[33] Before making such a transfer, be sure to check whether you will incur a surrender charge from your existing TSA provider. A portion of your existing TSA account may be free from surrender charges, and can be "rolled over" into a TSA life policy without cost.

[34] Under the 2001 Tax Act, beginning in 2002 the includible amount is further reduced.

[35] Statistical Abstracts of the United States, 2000 edition, p.84.

[36] The CPI-U index has since 1913 been used as a measure of the cost of an average "market basket" of goods and services purchased by urban Americans. Data from the Bureau of Labor website: ***ftp://ftp.bls.gov/pub/special.request/cpi/cpiai.txt***.

[37] See, for example, Markowitz, Harry, *Portfolio Selection: Efficient Diversification of Investments*, Blackwell Publishers, 1996.

[38] Source: Dow Jones Industrial Average, 1900 through June 30, 2001. The index is unmanaged. Number of declines assumes 0% recovery of lost value. Average length measures market high to low. Last occurrence marks the most recent market low.

[39] Source: American Funds Distributors, Inc. Lit. No. AFD-335-0901, © 2001. Results of hypothetical investments in Standard & Poor's 500 Composite Index, an unmanaged measure of relatively large U.S. companies, calculated with dividends taken in cash.

[40] It took investors 16 years to restore their investments in the 1929 market crash, if they invested at the market high. After the 1987 crash, it took 23 months to recover the original prices. In 1990 it took only eight months. All cases assume dividends were reinvested. Keep in mind, as always, that past performance does not predict future performance, and there is no guarantee that this market behavior will repeat in the future.

[41] Returns and volatility risk, as measured by standard deviation, 1/1/70-12/31/99. This assumes a single investment in 1970. Data from Ibbetson Associates, *Stocks, Bonds, Bills And Inflation*- Bonds: Salomon Smith Barney Long-Term High-Grade Corporate Bond Index; Stocks: the S&P 500. Chart courtesy of American Funds Distributors, Inc.

[42] Returns for 1/1/70-12/31/99 reflect weighted averages of the performance of unmanaged indexes used to represent each strategy's asset classes. Returns assume reinvestment of all distributions and are not based on the returns of specific investments. Each strategy is rebalanced to its original target percentages annually. The indexes are: Lipper Growth Fund Index (growth); Lipper Growth and Income Funds Index (growth & income); Salomon Smith Barney Long-Term High-grade Corporate Bond Index (income); U.S. Treasury Bill Index (cash equivalents); 1970-1976 from CRSP Government Bond File and 1977-1999 from *The Wall Street Journal*. Data from Lipper Inc.and Ibbetson Associates. Chart courtesy of American Funds Distributors, Inc. Past performance does not predict future results.

[43] Tax law constantly changes, which requires you to rethink and update your plans. However, if the estate tax repeal becomes permanent, some planning strategies described below would obviously become unnecessary. I urge readers to keep abreast of developments in this field, as these could have a profound impact on estate plans already in place.

[44] The exemption equivalent for gift tax remains at $1,000,000.

[45] The credit for estate taxes paid to a state will be reduced beginning in 2002 and eliminated in 2005-2009. There will be no deduction in 2010, when the estate tax is scheduled for a one-year repeal. The current estate tax credit is scheduled to reappear in 2011 and later, when the 2001 tax act ceases to be effective.

[46] Contributions to the trust to pay premiums are considered by the IRS to be future interest gifts instead of present interest gifts. Future interest gifts typically do not qualify for the $10,000 annual gift tax exclusion. This concern can be overcome by granting to the beneficiaries a limited power to withdraw certain sums from the trust for a short time after the grantor makes the contribution. This is sometimes referred to as a "Crummey provision" after the case that decided the validity of this technique (Crummey v. Commissioner, 397 F.2d 82 (9th Cir. 1968)). The rules set forth in this case and subsequent rulings must be carefully followed. "Crummey power" holders should be actual trust beneficiaries; however, the Tax Court allowed annual exclusions for contingent beneficiaries (e.g., children, grandchildren, etc.) who were given withdrawal rights (*Est. of Cristofani v. Commissioner*, 97 T.C. 74 (1991)). There are other rules concerning payments to the trust that must be followed. Make sure to consult a knowledgeable and competent attorney if you wish to create this type of trust.

[47] Part B is medical insurance that covers doctors' services, clinical laboratory services, outpatient hospital services and outpatient transfusions. Part B also covers preventative services, including Pap smear and pelvic exams, diabetes monitoring as well as other tests.

FOOTNOTES

[48] You may purchase Medigap (Medicare supplement) insurance, which will cover this "co-payment," and which can amount to $7,920.

[49] U.S. Code Reference 42 U.S.C. 1396p(d.

[50] *www.ssa.gov/cgi-bin/benefit.cgi.*

[51] You may call the Social Security Administration at 1-800-772-1213 for a personalized benefit estimate. You should indicate the age you expect to retire in your current projected earnings. You may want to apply for several statements to compare benefits at different retirement ages.

[52] IRA distributions will also not be counted as wages for the earnings test.

[53] Note that these rules apply to U.S. citizens and residents, and that different rules apply to individuals who are not U.S. citizens or residents. Nonresident aliens pay tax on 85% of social security benefits at the 30% rate unless a treaty applies.

ABOUT THE AUTHOR

Michael C. Franzblau is a retired public educator who for the past eighteen years has provided pre-and post-retirement financial strategies to educators. Each year he presents numerous seminars about financial issues to educators in the New York metropolitan region.

Dr. Franzblau earned a B.A. at Columbia College, and an M.A. and Ph.D. at Yale University. A physicist by training, in 1970 he joined the science faculty at Mamaroneck High School in Mamaroneck, NY, where he taught for twenty years. While at Mamaroneck High, he developed and directed the *School Within A School*, one of the first alternative high schools in the United States. This pioneering school was widely studied and became a model for other alternative schools throughout the U.S. In 1972, he created *Pinebrook Educational Group,* a teacher- training institute that conducted innovative graduate courses for more than 8,000 public school teachers in cooperation with regional universities. In 1989, Dr. Franzblau retired from teaching to work full-time in the financial services industry. He has helped many educators create and implement effective financial plans. You may contact Dr. Franzblau by writing to him at *Strategies for Wealth Creation and Protection*, 1025 Westchester Avenue, White Plains, New York 10604 or by e-mail at *mfranzblau@nepsusa.org.*

Index

Annual exclusion   142

Attorney,
   issues to consider before meeting   147
   powers of   156

Beliefs,
   utility of positive   164

Charitable bequests   160,161

CPI inflation   108,109

Dollar Cost Averaging   122

Efficient Market   114

Estate Planning
   popular instruments for   146,147
   probate process   144-146
   taxation of estate assets   141-144
   unified credit   142
   value of process   15,16,140

Executor
   choosing   149,150

Gifts
   taxation of   141,142

Guardian
   choosing   149

Health care proxy   147

Inflation
   effect on retirement income   106-109

Information for planner   169-171

Insurance,
   automobile   19-21
   disability income   28-30
   homeowners   21
   liability   20
   liability limits & deductibles   25,26
   life. (See Life Insurance)
   long-term care. (See Long-term care insurance)
   property and casualty   18,19
   umbrella liability   23

Life insurance,
   as income replacement   28
   cash values   92,96,97
   guarantees   34,37
   in 401B plan   99
   in pension planning   82-89,93
   permanent   36,84-87
   qualifying for   34,35
   Second-to-die   162
   survivorship life   162
   Tax-sheltered annuity life   99-104
   (TSA life insurance)
   term   94
   universal life   39
   variable universal life   41
   variable whole life   40
   whole life   37

Living Will   156

Long-term care
   and Medicaid   48,175-179
   and Medicare   48,173,174

Long-term care insurance,
benefit triggers 54
chance of needing 45
components of policy 49-51
features and benefits 49
how people pay for 46
introduction 43
qualifying for 52
tax deduction for premiums 56

Market Declines, history of 118

Medicaid 175-179

Medicare 173-174

Micro and Macro planning 5

Mutual Funds
cost to purchase and own 135,136
tax issues 137
types 131-135

Pension
Basics 67,68
how computed 81
maximum vs. joint-and-survivor
13,70,71
using life insurance 82-89

Pension options
declining reserve 73
joint-and-survivor 74
period certain 72

Planner
documents to assemble for 169-171

Pour-over will (see Wills, types)

Power of attorney, durable 156

Probate 144-146

QTIP trust (see Trusts, types)

Qualified Domestic trust (see Trusts, types)

Revocable trusts (see Trusts, types)

Second-to-die life insurance (see Life Insurance)

Social Security
age to qualify 182
benefit calculation 182,183
and early retirement 183,184
tax issues 186,187

Springing Durable Power of Attorney
for healthcare decisions 157

Survivorship life insurance (see Life Insurance)

Tax-sheltered annuity 99-101
life insurance within 100,104

Trusts, types
Credit Shelter Trust 158
Irrevocable trusts 154
QTIP Trust 155
Qualified Domestic Trust 155
Revocable trusts 152-154

TSA life insurance (see Life Insurance)

Unified credit 142,143

Wills. types
Living will 155
Pour-over will 154
Simple will 148